A Pre-Columbian Crusade to America

OTHER BOOKS BY HJALMAR HOLAND

History of the Norwegian Immigration, 1908 (three editions)

History of Door County, Wisconsin, 1917

Old Peninsula Days, 1925 (seven editions)

Coon Prairie, 1927 (two editions)

Coon Valley, 1928 (two editions)

The Last Migration, 1930

Wisconsin's Belgian Community, 1931

The Kensington Stone, 1932

Westward From Vinland, 1940 (three editions)

America, 1355-1364, 1946 (two editions)

Explorations in America Before Columbus, 1956

My First Eighty Years, 1957

A PRE-COLUMBIAN CRUSADE TO AMERICA

by Hjalmar R. Holand

Twayne Publishers, Inc.   ::   New York

Copyright © 1962 by Twayne Publishers, Inc.

Library of Congress Catalog Card Number 62-13675

MANUFACTURED IN THE UNITED STATES OF AMERICA BY
UNITED PRINTING SERVICES, INC.
NEW HAVEN, CONN.

CONTENTS

CONTENTS

LIST OF ILLUSTRATIONS

INTRODUCTION

Exactly six hundred years ago, thirty white men camped on the bank of Nelson River, near Hudson Bay.

They came not to seek gold or capture slaves. These thirty men from the Scandinavian Peninsula—many of them members of the Royal Norse Bodyguard—had been chosen by their king, Magnus Erikson, for a very special and noble purpose. Word had reached him that a large group of Norsemen in Greenland, overwhelmed by the sneaking attacks of countless Eskimo and forgotten by their king, had left their homes, given up the Christian faith, and emigrated to that highly praised land in the West which their ancestors had discovered and called Vinland.

Filled with self-reproach, the king, who was an ardent supporter of the Church, fitted out an expedition for the purpose of bringing these unfortunate Greenlanders back into the Church. In 1363 or possibly in 1364, eight survivors of this expedition returned to Norway and reported that they had reached an inland sea not far from the magnetic pole. They had not found the alleged apostates. They also reported that Greenland was without a bishop, the last incumbent having died fifteen years previously.

In 1898, an illiterate Swedish pioneer near Kensington, Minnesota, made a strange discovery. While clearing land for the plow, he found a large flat stone beneath a tree and clutched in its roots. This stone contained a long inscription which was first thought to be in Greek letters. Later it was found that the more than two hundred characters were runic letters. However, none of the scholars in American or European universities who at that time inspected the stone or saw copies of the inscription was able to make a complete translation. The numerals on the stone, which gave its date, were particularly baffling and were thought to be an invention of the man who had made the inscription. Moreover, the fact that this inscription was found in western Minnesota, near the geographical center of the North American continent, was also considered highly questionable. As these critics were highly respected scholars, there was no one who questioned their verdict, at least not publicly. The inscription was dead!

My knowledge of the stone did not come until nine years later when I chanced to visit Kensington and saw the stone. I had some knowledge of runic writing, and translated the whole inscription. The question of what lay behind it aroused my curiosity, and its study became my principal occupation, resulting in the writing and publication of five books. In the meantime the Minnesota Historical Society became interested and requested a committee of five scholars to investigate the circumstances of the discovery of the stone. These men spent a year and a half in thorough research and then published a unanimous report that the inscription was authentic. This report of 68 printed pages was the first detailed discussion about the stone. It was met by much opposition, and the committee took the question up for renewed consideration. Three years later the committee published a new report which again, unanimously, affirmed the authenticity of the inscription. The subject was also elucidated by a number of scholars who wrote lengthy monographs defending the inscription. Among these may be mentioned Professor Andrew Fossum, St. Olaf College, Northfield, Minn.; Professor William Thalbitzer, University of Denmark, and Professor S. N. Hagen in *Speculum*.

There were also many articles from the negative side, but very brief. Only one small volume against the inscription has been published. This is by Professor Erik Wahlgren, University of Southern California, entitled *The Kensington Stone, A Mystery Solved*. However, as this book is a veritable hailstorm of derogatory personalities, it has not won any laurels for its author.

The last ten years have been very productive in new discoveries proving the authenticity of the Kensington inscription. For this reason this new book is by far the most important of the five I have written on this subject. We have found no less than fifteen of the campsites of these explorers, beginning on Lake Winnipeg and continuing down among the many lakes of northwestern Minnesota, so that we are now able to follow their route from day to day. We have also found more than a dozen of their arms and implements. Best of all was the discovery in the British Museum of a long report on Nicholas of Lynn's discovery of Hudson Bay in the 1360's. He spent two years there, 1362 and 1363, and then returned to Greenland and Norway. This report also mentions that the expedition of which he was a member divided in two, thus giving him plenty of time for exploration. This division of the expedition is also mentioned on the Kensington Stone. It says that twenty men went inland, leaving ten men in charge of the ships.

H. R. HOLAND

A Pre-Columbian Crusade to America

chapter one

GREENLAND

In 982 A.D. a man accused of manslaughter appeared before a court in Iceland. Since he was a stranger from Norway without many friends, there was not much chance of his getting a fair trial. He was found guilty and declared an outlaw for three years. This meant that anyone could kill him during that period without fear of prosecution. His name was Erik Thorwaldson.

In those days, freebooting was considered almost a gentlemanly occupation, and as Erik had a ship and was a valiant man with much self-reliance, it is possible that he considered this course. But he was a married man with four small children, and they would be much in the way in a fight at sea. He therefore decided to seek a new land in the unknown West. He secreted his wife and children and readied his ship with the help of friends. Then, with his family, he sailed toward the setting sun.

Several hundred miles to the west of Iceland he found a new land. But this land was stern and glaciated and flanked by vast fields of slowly moving ice. He followed it southward many hundred miles without finding an opening to the shore. Finally he rounded an icy promontory now known as Cape Farewell, and around on the other side he found a better land. Here were fields of luxuriant grass, reindeer on the hills, seals without number on the rocks along the shore, and great whales spouting in the offing. He traveled far and wide and spent three years in exploring this land which seemed very good to him.

In 985 he returned to Iceland and found that sentiment toward him had changed greatly. He was now treated as an honored guest, and people flocked together wherever he stayed to hear him tell of this new land. He called it Greenland because, as he said, a good land should have a good name. He said he was going back the next year, and there was plenty of land for those who wanted to join him. When he returned to Greenland the following year, there were no less than twenty-five vessels filled with emigrants who joined him. Unfortunately, they ran into a bad storm, and eleven ships were lost with all on board.

This was the beginning of the first republic in the West. Erik was the recognized governor, but without a title. He owned millions of acres of land, mining rights, and fishing and hunting privileges. He paid no taxes because no government claimed sovereignty. In turn, he gave thousands of acres to his friends and asked for no rents. With these favorable conditions, the colony grew rapidly, and in a generation or two it numbered about three thousand people. They were divided in two settlements, both on the southwest side of Greenland. One lay just northwest of Cape Farewell. It had twelve parishes with two monasteries, a nunnery and an imposing cathedral. This was known as the Eastern Settlement. About 250 miles beyond the western frontier was a smaller colony known as the Western Settlement. This had four parishes.

For three hundred years and more this republic enjoyed a peaceful and prosperous existence. While no cereals could be grown, Greenland, like Iceland, had good grazing lands for cows and sheep. The latter produced wool which was woven into wadmal and shipped to Europe in large quantities.

It was not long before it was discovered that Greenland had other sources of wealth. It was not only the abundance of seals, which produced favorite furs then as now. The tusks of the walrus were a good substitute for ivory, and the Greenlanders produced so much of it that elephant tusks were almost pushed off the market. Eiderdown also brought a big price. The Greenland falcons were superior to all others, and were eagerly sought by the rich from Bergen to Baghdad. Finally there were the polar bears, which when captured young were easily tamed. Such a tame bear was considered so desirable a pet that it brought a fabulous price. Usually no price was placed on such an animal. Instead, it was presented to some king who in return would make a big present to the man who brought it. Several instances are recorded of a man presenting a polar bear to a king and getting not only a ship but a cargo of timber in return.

There was therefore a time when Greenland was a prosperous community. Evidences of this prosperity are seen in the remains of huge farmhouses and barns. Much timber was needed for roof construction and for ships, furniture, coffins and a hundred other things made of wood. As it was only one-third as far from Greenland to Newfoundland as from Greenland to Norway, it is probable that most of the Greenlander's timber was obtained from Newfoundland. The Greenland records are lost, but we know through Icelandic channels of at least eight ships bound for Greenland and loaded with timber from Markland (i.e., timber land), by which was meant Nova Scotia and Newfoundland.

Such were the conditions in this peaceful republic during its first three hundred years. But in the middle of the thirteenth century, Norway had an ambitious monarch who wanted to enlarge his dominions by taking over all the western islands. Through his persuasion, Greenland and Iceland became colonial possessions of Norway in 1261. At first, this union did not interfere with the Greenland trade, because there were many men there who sailed their own ships and thus were free to carry on as before. But in 1294 a strict order was issued prohibiting any sailings to and from Greenland without a royal license. This was chiefly intended to stop the Hanseatic League, whose aggressive trading practices made life miserable for the governments of Norway and Denmark; but private commerce became more and more difficult. It was particularly onerous to the Western Settlement. The royal freight vessel, on arriving in Greenland, would put in at the Eastern Settlement which was much the better and more populous market; the insufficient imports would quickly be bought up, and there would be nothing left for the Western Settlement.

Another great evil was the irregularity of the sailings of the royal vessels. This is shown by the long lapses between the deaths of the bishops and the installation of their successors—normally a prompt step because collection of taxes depended on the energy of the bishop. Thus Bishop Olaf, dying in 1280, was not replaced until 1288. Again, the death of Bishop Arni in 1349 was not learned in Norway until 1364.

We know little of the relations between the Greenlanders and the Eskimo during the earlier period of Greenland history. But it was inevitable that hostilities would break out between the Northmen and the Eskimo because of their competition for the same hunting grounds.

At first the trouble was confined to the Western Settlement. Presumably the Eskimo made no attack in force; instead they resorted to sniping. The Norsemen lived on large, scattered farms, separated by ridges and marshes, and their cattle and sheep strayed far. It was easy for a small band of Eskimo to kill some of the stock, set fire to the haystacks far from the farmhouse, and ambush any lone man they could find. Whatever the chain of events, the day came in 1342 when the Western Settlement was found to be abandoned. It is said to have numbered ninety farms, and the population may have been somewhere between six and nine hundred people.

This exodus is told by an eyewitness, Father Ivar Bardson, a Norse Greenlander, at that time. In 1341 he was sent to Greenland by Bishop Haakon of Bergen who was an old friend of Bishop Arni in Greenland. As Bishop Haakon had not heard from his friend for many years, he fitted out a ship at his own expense and dispatched Father Ivar of Greenland with greetings and many presents. Ivar reached Greenland in safety and found the Bishop alive, but very old and feeble. At the Bishop's request Father Ivar remained there as steward of the Church properties for many years. In Greenland he learned that the people of the Western Settlement were having trouble with the Eskimo, and the next year, 1342, he went with a company of men to see if they could be of any help to their countrymen in the Western Settlement. The following is a recorded part of his report dealing with this mission:

> . . . There in the Western Settlement stands a large Church which is called Sandnes Church, which, for a time was a cathedral and episcopal see; but now the Scraelings

have occupied all the Western Settlement, there are many horses, goats, cows and sheep, all wild, but no people, neither Christian nor heathen. All this was told us by Ivar Bardson Greenlander, who was in charge of the episcopal see at Gardar for many years. He had seen all this, and he was one of those appointed by the Lawspeaker to sail to the Western Settlement against the Scraelings and drive them out. But when they came thither they found no one, neither Christian nor heathen, nothing but some wild sheep and cattle. They took what was needed to feed the men and loaded as many as the ships could hold and then sailed home.[1]

There has been much discussion as to what became of these people of the Western Settlement. Some writers have thought that they were exterminated by the Eskimo. But as Ivar Bardson does not mention any signs of bloodshed, this theory is without support. Besides, as Frithjof Nansen says: "Can anyone who knows the Eskimo imagine that they slaughtered the men but not the cattle? These represented food for them, and that is what they would first turn their attention to."

But while he properly rejects this theory, Nansen proposes another even more unlikely. He thinks that Ivar Bardson and his men arrived in the Western Settlement just at a time when the Northmen voluntarily gave up their accustomed mode of life and joined the Eskimo. He assumes that the Northmen eventually would come to the conclusion that Greenland was better adapted for hunting than for agriculture.

This does not sound reasonable. The Northmen were no inexperienced newcomers to Greenland. Ten generations had lived there, and they had learned how to get the most out of the circumstances in which they lived by a combination of animal husbandry and the hunting of seals, walrus and whales. They would gain nothing by taking up the life of the Eskimo, and they would lose their native dairy diet and their large comfortable homes. And what would the Eskimo think of the intrusion of hundreds of white men into the humble economy of their life? Up to this time the Northmen had been only part-time hunters; if they gave up their agronomy and spent all their time hunting, the enmity between the two races would be more bitter than ever. In view of this complete helplessness, there was only one thing for the Greenland Norsemen to do, and that was to seek refuge in that great land to the southwest where their countrymen and their bishop had gone long ago, as recorded in the old annals. The plan was not without danger, but it may have seemed promising to them.

This exodus did not become known in Norway or Iceland for several years. Then in 1347 a ship with eighteen men from the Eastern Settlement set out for Markland on one of the periodic voyages for timber. On their return late in the season they were driven to Iceland. Here they reported the important news that the people of the Western Settlement had moved away—no one knew where. This came to the attention of John Guthormson, a prominent Icelandic chief. He found lodgings for these men, and in the spring he took them to the king to whom they told the story of the evacuation of the Western Settlement.[2]

This exodus was also recorded in the Annals of Skalholt, the principal episcopal see in Iceland. This was the main repository in Iceland for church records. In 1630 this episcopal see was destroyed by fire. Bishop Gisle Oddson had spent all his life there since he was son of the former bishop. After the fire he attempted to make a synopsis in Latin of some of the more important documents that he could remember. Among these was the report of the disappearance of the people of the Western Settlement in Greenland. This is what he wrote:[3]

> 1342. The inhabitants of Greenland fell voluntarily away from the true faith and the Christian religion, and after having given up all good manners and true virtues, turned to the people of America (*ad Americae populos se converterunt*). Some say that Greenland lies very near the western lands of the world.

Some commentators have pointed to the clause *ad Americae populos se converterunt* as evidence that the emigrants united with the Eskimo. But this imputes to the Bishop an anachronism of speech. As John Fiske says in his introduction to his *Discovery of America:* "In dealing with the discovery of America one must steadily keep before one's mind the quaint notions of ancient geographers." When the Bishop said America, he meant, of course, *continental* America. No one, even now, would think of alluding to the Eskimo of Greenland as people of America. Then he adds: "Some say that Greenland lies very near to the western lands of the world." It is as if he had said: "They probably had not far to go, because it is said that Greenland lies very near to America." Professor P. A. Munch is entirely of the same view. He says: "The attacks of the Eskimo were presumably the cause of what is stated in an annalistic notice of 1342, to wit, that the inhabitants of (Western) Greenland fell voluntarily from Christianity and emigrated to America. . . . This account has all the evidence of truth."[4]

chapter two

KING MAGNUS ORDERS AN EXPEDITION
TO SEARCH FOR LOST COLONISTS

In the middle of the fourteenth century, Norway and Sweden were ruled jointly by King Magnus Erikson. The people of Norway were conservative and looked with doubt upon entanglements with other countries, and the Royal Council insisted on a proviso that the union with Sweden should come to an end when Haakon, the king's second son, reached his majority in 1355.

Nor was Magnus popular in Sweden where, taking the part of the common people, he antagonized a strong aristocracy which resisted any reductions in its ancient privileges. These aristocrats persuaded his other son, Erik, to rise in rebellion against his father. Most of the leading men in every province in Sweden except one (West Gothland) turned against King Magnus. He was a descendant of the Folkunga family, the leading family in West Gothland, and it was natural that he favored the people of this province. He appointed many of their sons to his royal bodyguard —the first important step toward knighthood. So loyal were the people of this province that they refused to be called Swedes. Instead they called themselves Goths.

King Magnus had one great ambition. This was to compel the Russians to accept the Roman Catholic faith. He persuaded the Pope, Clement VI, to endorse this enterprise, and the latter ordered a crusade against Russia to be preached in Prussia, Poland and the Scandinavian countries. With this backing the king went ahead, enlisting men, building ships, and providing an ample commissariat. Then in 1348, just as he was ready to put to sea, the Icelandic chief, Jon Guthormson and the eighteen men from Greenland came to see him. They came with the startling news that many hundreds of his subjects in faraway Greenland had given up the Christian faith.

This was a shocking piece of news, but what could the king do? Just then there was nothing else but to proceed with his campaign because many thousands of men were already on their way to Russia. So he sailed with his army, captured a big fortress, and compelled hundreds of Russians, under the threat of death, to be baptized. Then, leaving a large garrison in charge of the fortress, he returned home. But the Russians reassembled in countless number, recaptured the fortress after a siege of six months, and put the members of the garrison to death.

The king had no intention of dropping his crusade because of this disaster. But simultaneously came a report from the western part of Norway that a pestilence had broken out which threatened to exterminate the entire population. This was the terrible Black Death, which in the middle of the fourteenth century spread over all Europe and Asia, killing many millions of people. Men and women were dying in almost every house, and many people thought the world was coming to an end.

This terrible catastrophe did not stop, but only delayed the king's attempt to convert the Russians. He sent a delegation to the Pope asking for funds to continue the war. Then, without waiting for an answer, he set out with another army in 1351. This campaign, though partly successful, was more disastrous than the former, and when he returned the next year, he had lost many men and all his financial resources.

On his return in 1352 he was met with good news. The Pope had hearkened to his request and sent word to King Magnus that he could keep half of the tithe money collected in Sweden and Norway for the next four years.

Full of cheer, the king prepared for another campaign in 1353. But now the report was heard that the plague had reached Russia, and as the Northmen believed it would be suicidal to expose themselves to it again, they refused any inducements to take part in the proposed crusade.

Bitterly disappointed, the king was now reminded of the bad situation in Greenland. In his ardor to be a great crusader for the Church, he had neglected his people in Greenland, and he was deeply remorseful, as is shown by his letter of command (see below). Fortunately he had the funds provided through the cooperation of the Pope, and, seeing he could not go east, he decided to go west. We have a copy of a letter issued by him late in 1354, in which he provides for an extraordinary expedition to Greenland. At its head is placed Paul Knutson, formerly Chief Justice of the District of Gulathing. The following is a translation of the letter:

MAGNUS, BY THE GRACE OF GOD, KING OF NORWAY, SWEDEN AND SKAANE, SENDS TO ALL MEN WHO SEE OR HEAR THIS LETTER GOOD HEALTH AND HAPPINESS.

WE DESIRE TO MAKE KNOWN TO YOU THAT YOU [PAUL KNUTSON] ARE TO TAKE THE MEN WHO SHALL GO IN THE KNORR [THE ROYAL TRADING VESSEL] WHETHER THEY BE NAMED OR NOT NAMED, . . . FROM MY BODYGUARD AND ALSO FROM AMONG THE RETAINERS OF OTHER MEN WHOM YOU MAY WISH TO TAKE ON THE VOYAGE WHO ARE BEST QUALIFIED TO ACCOMPANY HIM, WHETHER AS OFFICERS OR MEN. WE ASK THAT YOU ACCEPT THIS OUR COMMAND WITH A RIGHT GOOD WILL FOR THE CAUSE, INASMUCH AS WE DO IT FOR THE HONOR OF GOD, AND *for the sake of our soul,* AND FOR THE SAKE OF OUR PREDECESSORS WHO IN GREENLAND ESTABLISHED CHRISTIANITY AND HAVE MAINTAINED IT UNTIL THIS TIME, AND WE WILL NOT LET IT PERISH IN OUR DAYS. KNOW THIS FOR TRUTH, THAT WHOEVER DEFIES THIS OUR COMMAND SHALL MEET WITH OUR SERIOUS DISPLEASURE AND RECEIVE FULL PUNISHMENT. [Italics added.]

EXECUTED IN BERGEN, MONDAY AFTER SIMON AND JUDAH'S DAY IN THE SIX AND THIRTIETH YEAR OF OUR RULE (1354). BY ORM OSTENSON, OUR REGENT, SEALED.[1]

Briefly, the purpose of this expedition was to reestablish Christianity in Greenland, which was its first destination as the place where this relapse into heathenism had taken place. If the apostates were not there, it would be necessary to follow them where they had gone. The expedition was not in any way concerned with commercial activity. The king's soul as well as the spiritual welfare of his western subjects was at stake. A man of the highest standing in the kingdom was chosen, with authority to conscript the best men he could find.

We have no direct report on the result of this expedition, and some critics have therefore assumed that it never took place. But this shows a failure to understand the religious fervor of the times. A king who was so alarmed about the eternal welfare of a people of another nation that he spent large sums of money to teach them the "true faith," surely would not be indifferent to the fact that his own people were becoming idolators. His emphatic letter to Sir Paul Knutson shows that he was profoundly disturbed about the matter.

Apparently no one in modern times paid much attention to this 1354 letter or mandate of the king until near the beginning of the present century. Professor Gustav Storm, the historian, was the first to see the significance of it. In 1888 he wrote the following:

> We have a copy of a royal letter from Oktober, 1354, which indicates extraordinary preparations. Paul Knutson of Onarheim, a member of the King's Bodyguard, is appointed leader of the expedition, and he is given special authority to fit it out and choose the members of it. The purpose of the enterprise is stated to be "to maintain Christianity in Greenland," that is, to fight the Eskimo and to strengthen the colony in general, perhaps also to explore the new lands. In any case we can be sure that the conditions in Greenland and its fate were in those years debated in Bergen, from whence the expedition departed, and where, after a number of years, it returned. We know that it had not returned in 1357. It appears most probable that it did not return until 1363 or 1364, because in the last year Ivar Bardson reappears again, and not before 1365 is a new bishop to Greenland consecrated.[2]

There was another great historian long before Gustav Storm who added something of importance to the record of this expedition. This was Archbishop Olaus Magnus who, while living in exile in Rome, wrote a great work on the history and mode of life on the Scandinavian peninsula. He writes:[3]

[In Greenland] live a kind of pirates who make use of a kind of skin boat . . . in which they attack merchant vessels, seeking to sink them by piercing their hulls from below instead of attacking them from above. In the year 1505 I personally saw two of these skin boats above the western portal within the cathedral dedicated to the sainted Halvard, where they were put on the wall for general exhibition. It is stated that King Haakon captured them when he with his battle fleet passed the coast of Greenland just as they [the natives] prepared to sink his vessel in the sea.

This passage is highly significant. It was, of course, an error when someone in the church told the future archbishop (then fifteen years old) that King Haakon had personally commanded this expedition. The years of his reign, 1355-80, were filled with wars and intrigues, first with the Hanseatic League and then with King Albrecht, a foreign claimant to his throne. Professor Munch's very complete biography shows that King Haakon did not once leave the Scandinavian countries. Divested of this embellishment, the information conveyed is that a royal naval expedition operated in the Greenland waters some time in King Haakon's reign; and that it was not of commercial nature but sailed in war vessels. What could be better so described than the Paul Knutson expedition? It took place in King Haakon's time,[4] it was a royal expedition sent to Greenland, and it was not of commercial nature. It was easy for oral tradition to dramatize this expedition for the redemption of the Greenland apostates into a royal battle fleet with the king himself in command.

But why did the Bishop of Oslo give these Eskimo kayaks a place of honor in the great cathedral? Certainly the capture of two one-man canoes was not such a great naval victory that it was worthy of such a distinguished commemoration. Professor Munch is probably right when he assumes that the kayaks were placed on the wall of the cathedral by command of King Haakon, who had good reasons for doing so. The same year (1364) that the survivors of the Paul Knutson expedition returned, the sovereignty of Sweden was lost to Magnus and Haakon when the Swedish nobles chose Albrecht Albrechtson of Mechlenburg as king. The following year King Magnus was captured by King Albrecht and languished in prison for six years. King Haakon had a very difficult time in raising the huge ransom demanded—more than a million dollars in today's money .

Quite understandably, he would place the kayaks in the cathedral to remind the people of his father's pious enterprise in trying to save the apostate Greenlanders from damnation.[5] Thus, he obtained not only the contributions, but also the prayers of his people for his father's liberation. Indeed, he was so successful in building up his father's reputation for good works that when King Magnus perished at sea two years later, he was worshiped as a national saint.[6]

This expedition was authorized on one of the last days of October, 1354. It is therefore doubtful if it would be ready to sail in the spring or summer of 1355. In any case it probably did not sail until 1356 because it is recorded that the year 1355 was so stormy that no ships came to or departed from Iceland that year, as recorded in the Icelandic Annals.

chapter three

THE DISCOVERY AND REJECTION OF
THE KENSINGTON STONE

The history of Minnesota does not go back very far. A few scattered fur traders pushed up its rivers in Indian canoes in the eighteenth century, but as it was the home of the warlike Sioux, the progress was slow. In 1820, Fort Snelling was built at the junction of Minnesota River with the Mississippi, and this was for a long time the lone gateway to the unknown North. Although the soil in the greater part of Minnesota is of excellent quality, its first farmers did not come until about the middle of the nineteenth century. Then, in 1849, the Territory of Minnesota was organized and the settlement of the southeastern part of the future state began.

The village of Kensington is in the southwestern corner of Douglas County in the west-central part of Minnesota. To the north and east lies the great lake-park region of Minnesota, to the west and south stretches the endless prairie.

Not until 1867 did the first settlers begin to appear in the Kensington area—a few hardy pioneers willing to take up land several days' journey beyound the nearest railroad point. It was mostly second-rate farm land with many moraines and swamps, and in consequence the settlement grew slowly. Twenty years passed before the pioneers were able to start a school. The land on which the Kensington stone was found was not settled until 1891, when a man named Olof Ohman took possession of it. This farm consisted of three rather steep hills and a large expanse of marsh (see Figure 2).

One day in November, 1898, this man was engaged in clearing land in the southeastern corner of his farm. This spot was about three-quarters of a mile from his own house, but only a quarter mile from the buildings of his neighbor to the east, with an open marsh between Ohman's hilltop and his neighbor's barn.

Ohman had recently come from Sweden where he had learned how to get rid of a tree and its main roots in one operation. First he dug a trench a few feet from the tree and around it and cut all its horizontal roots. Then he attached a block and tackle to the tree as high up as possible. A second block was anchored to the base of another tree, and thus sufficient power was gained not only to pull down the tree, but also to pull up its roots. In digging away the soil brought up with the roots of one such tree, he found that a large flat stone was held firmly by its two main roots. This stone carried a long inscription in strange characters but in regularly spaced lines. (Figure 1.)

Nils Flaten, the neighbor, was cutting brush on his own land only a few rods away, and he came over from time to time to see Ohman pull down the trees. He saw the stone as soon as it was liberated from the big roots that held it and also the inscription. He brought the news to Kensington, and before long the theory was evolved that someone—a robber, perhaps—must have buried a treasure there and made some mystic marks on the stone to mark the spot. With Ohman's permission, a big hole, seven feet deep and wide, was dug, but nothing was found but an antique whetstone, so worn with use that it broke in two. These pieces were thrown back into the hole which was filled up. Since Ohman soon tired of answering questions, he removed the stone from the roots and took it to Kensington, where it was placed on exhibition in the window of the one-man bank there.

Unlike modern villages, Kensington had no scholarly recluse who could cast light on a mysterious inscription. But in every community there are usually a few men who gain some respect for knowing more than others. Kensington had three such men. One was J. P. Hedberg, a Swede, who had a small real estate business and sold steamship tickets and insurance. He was sure the inscription was written in Greek letters. Another was S. A. Siverts, the cashier in the bank, who also leaned toward the

Greek theory. The third was Samuel Olson, a jeweler and optician. He did not know what to think.

After almost two months of discussion, these three men decided to do something about the inscription. Mr. Hedberg had great faith in the omniscience of the editor of the Swedish newspaper, *Svenska Amerikanska Posten*, published in Minneapolis, and he wrote the following letter:

Kensington, Minn., Jan. 1, 1899.

SWAN J. TURNBLAD
MINNEAPOLIS

I enclose you a copy of an inskription on a stone found about 2 miles from Kensington by a O. Ohman he found it under a tree when Grubbing—he wanted I should go out and look at it and I told him to haul it in when he came (not thinking much of it) and he did so, and this is an excest copy of it the first part is of the flat side of the stone the other was on flat edge. I thought I would send it to you as you perhaps have means to find out what it is—it appears to be old Greek letters please let me hear from you and oblige.

Yours truly

J. P. HEDBERG

The editor apparently had his doubt about whether or not there was such a find and filed the letter and copy away without a reply.

About the same time Mr. Siverts, the Norwegian bank cashier, made a good copy of the inscription. As he had little faith in the Swedish editor, he sent it to the professor of Greek at the University of Minnesota. The latter thought it might be runic and gave it to O. J. Breda, professor of Scandinavian languages. Six weeks later he presented the following translation:[1]

—— Swedes and —— Norwegians on a journey of discovery from Vinland west. We camped one day's journey north from this stone. We fished one day. After we came home we found —— men red with blood and dead A V M save from ——— Have ——— man at the sea to look after our ships ——— days journey from this island. Year ———

As Breda was unable to read the numerals, he missed the important date at the end of the inscription, 1362. Instead, as he says elsewhere, he thought it purported to tell something about the early eleventh-century discovery of America. He made no investigation of the circumstances of the discovery, and did not visit Kensington, nor did he ask any geologist to examine the weathering of the inscription.

In the meantime Samuel Olson in Kensington had obtained Ohman's permission to send the stone to Professor George O. Curme, chairman of the Germanic department of Northwestern University. Ten years later Curme told me he had had the stone in his study for two weeks. At first he was inclined to believe that the inscription was authentic and published a couple of statements to that effect. But finally he yielded to Breda's argumentation that this inscription should have been written in Old Norse. He expressed the view, however, that the weathering of the inscription indicated that it was carved several hundred years ago.[2]

A copy of the inscription was also sent to Norway where it came to the attention of Oluf Rygh, professor of Archaeology at the University of Oslo. He had an article about it in *Morgenbladet* about March 12, 1899. The following is Rygh's report:

The fabricator reveals himself to be a Swedish American who has become somewhat americanized. Some English words have escaped him here and there. He has used several uncommon signs; where he has found them is uncertain, but in any event they speak against, not for the authenticity of the inscription. Perhaps he has himself invented these signs. In some instances he uses the same sign for two sounds for a and ä, and o and å, sometimes he uses a wrong sign. As far as I can see, the inscription reads [translated]: ——— Goths and 22 Norwegians on a voyage of discovery from western Vinland. We had camp ——— 2 sleighs one days journey from this stone. We were and fished one day. After we came home we found 5 men red with blood and dead A V M. Have 5 men by the sea to look after our ships 14 days journey from this island year 1462.

The most uncertain is the significance of A V M and the three following words and the numerals, especially that which is read 5 and the second cipher in the number of the year.

Rygh's uncertainty about the meaning of the numerals reveals how little was known in 1899 about runic lore. Rygh was an expert archaeologist, but he was apparently unfamiliar with runic numerals which, as Ole Worm tells us in his Latin work, *Fasti Danici*, published in 1643, had been in use in 1328.[3]

In review of this translation, Professor S. N. Hagen writes:[4]

> It is to be observed that Rygh did much better than Breda in that he was able to read most of the numerals correctly. He omits 8 at the beginning, reads 5 for 10 (twice), and 1462 for 1362. The phrase *fro Vinland of west* he renders 'fra vestre Vinland' (from western Vinland). In the original text of the inscription which he gives with his translation, he reads *fard* for *farþ*, 2 *sklear* ('two sleds') for 2 *skjar, rese* (twice) for *rise, from* for *fro* in line 2, *dene* for *deno, rohde* for *röþ, illge* for *illy, åhr* for *ahr*. He twice identifies *from* with Eng. *from, of* (in *of west*) with Eng. *of*, and *ded* (his transliteration of *þeþ*) with Eng. *dead*.

In view of Rygh's reputation, his conclusion was accepted as final. Moreover, it was reported that he and Professor Gustav Storm sent a cablegram to some one in the United States that the inscription was "a grand fraud perpetrated by a Swede with a chisel and a slight knowledge of runic characters and of English." That such a cablegram was ever sent has never been verified. But the newspaper report of it was fatal to any credence which had been placed in the Kensington chronicle. After a few months of excited attention, the inscription was as dead as last year's weather reports.

chapter four

THE STONE IS RESURRECTED

At the time these things happened, I was a graduate student at the University of Wisconsin, studying for my Master's degree, and working during each summer as a traveling salesman. As such I visited many Norwegian-American settlements, and I learned much about the early Norwegian pioneers. Several articles of mine were published in newspapers and magazines.

In the winter of 1902 a call was issued for a meeting in Minneapolis to organize a cultural society, one of whose purposes was to preserve the history of the Norwegian pioneers. Attending this meeting, I was named archivist and historian of the new society, known as The Norwegian Society. My work was to visit Norwegian settlements and gather historical information. I prepared some talks on the subject of the pioneers, and the collections that were taken up were sufficient for my needs. Usually I spent several days in each parish or settlement in order to interview all the old settlers, and I also signed up many hundreds of new members. This society was very active for many years and regularly published a quarterly.

Traveling thus from settlement to settlement, I gathered many notebooks full of reminiscences by the pioneers. These were amplified by notes from church records in the keeping of the respective pastors. It was slow but gratifying work because I was writing the saga of the Norwegian immigration to America.[1]

Among the later settlements which I visited was a small group of Norwegians and Swedes in Douglas County near the small village of Kensington. This settlement was started in 1867, but as it was in a somewhat rough and swampy region, it did not prosper. Upon inquiring for things of historical interest, I found that the people had nothing to tell except that a stone had been found with some writing on it. This seemed highly mysterious, and I went to see Mr. Ohman, the finder of the stone. This was in 1907.

I found him to be a tall, well-built man of about fifty years with a frank and rugged countenance and a quiet dignity. I did not at first mention the inscribed stone, but told him of my work in gathering information about the early settlers and got him to talk about his own experiences. He was from Helsingland in the northern half of Sweden, where the school year in his youth was only six weeks long. He had had six of those years, making a total schooling of less than nine months. He was born in 1855 and in 1881 he emigrated to America and worked as a laborer among the farmers in Douglas County. In 1891 he was able to buy a small tract of wild land where he settled.

I asked him about the stone with writing on it, and he took me to his granary. On the ground, near the door, lay a large, flat stone, almost three feet long. He turned it over and took from the granary an old broom, with which he swept off most of the dirt on the surface. To my amazement I saw that more than half of the face of the stone was covered with very neatly carved characters. I recognized them as runic signs, because I had pondered over many runic inscriptions in my favorite study of Norse antiquities. Upon inquiry, he told me how he had found the stone. It was near the top of a fifty-foot knoll in the other end of his farm where he was grubbing trees. In grubbing out one of these trees, he had brought to light this stone, as described above. Ohman said that copies of the inscription had been sent to some learned men, but he understood that they "did not believe in the stone."

Well, that seemed to be all that Ohman could tell me. I could well understand that the inscription was rejected as a fraud, seeing it was found more than a thousand miles from the Atlantic coast. But who could have inscribed it? Here was a puzzle the solution of which had some promise. I asked Ohman for information about possibly learned persons with peculiar ideas, but he knew of none. "I know them all," he said, "and they are all just plain people like myself."

As I stood there inspecting this long inscription so neatly chiseled on the hard stone, I became more and more interested. In 1898 when the stone was found, the knowledge of runes was a long forgotten art, known only to a few experts in the Scandinavian universities. Aside from these few there was probably not one in a hundred thousand or even five-hundred thousand who could read or write runes. Yet here, in the far west pioneer region, someone had written an inscription containing several hundred characters! Who was this phenomenal person?

Could it be that the inscription was of ancient times? But no, that seemed impossible. According to Ohman, it had been rejected, and the idea of a company of men penetrating more than a thousand miles inland was preposterous. If the stone had been found on the eastern coast, the circumstances would have been quite different.

In my many years of traveling in the Norwegian settlements, I had obtained many interesting souvenirs from the pioneers. Here was the most interesting souvenir of all, and I wanted to have it very much. I told Mr. Ohman that I had studied runes in college and wanted very much to study the inscription, although I was now "rusty" in that field. The result was that after a little discussion he gave me the stone.

I went to Minneapolis and St. Paul and looked up some of the newspaper reports concerning the discovery of the stone nine years earlier and its rejestion by scholars. When I arrived at my home in eastern Wisconsin, I found that the stone had arrived in good condition. The accompanying figure shows my transcription of its message, line for line (see Figure 3):

1. (wi er) 8 göter ok 22 norrmen po
2. (en) opdagelsefarþ fro
3. winlanþ of west wi
4. haþe læger weþ 2 skjar en
5. þags rise norr fro þeno sten
6. wi war (ute) ok fiske en þagh æptir
7. we kom hem fan (wi) 10 man röde
8. af bloþ og ded A V M

   9. fræelse (os) av illy
  10. (wi) har 10 mans we (þ) hawet at se
  11. æptir wore skip 14 þagh rise
  12. from þeno öh (æptir guz byrþ) 1362

The translation is as follows. The words in *brackets* are omitted in the inscription.

> [We are] 8 Goths and 22 Norwegians on [an] exploration voyage from Vinland through the west we had camp by [a lake with] 2 skerries one day's voyage north from this stone we were [out] and fished one day after we came home [we] found 10 men red with blood and dead A[ve] M[aria] save [us] from evil [we] have 10 men by the sea to look after our ships 14 day voyages from this island [in the] year [of our Lord] 1362 (see Figure 3).

This first complete translation was published in *Skandina-ven*, a Norwegian newspaper, January, 1908. This article revived the subject because the date showed how completely at sea Professor Breda was when he claimed that the inscription had something to do with Leif Erikson about the year 1000. While this did not prove the authenticity of the inscription, it showed that it had been condemned on false evidence. It also awakened an interest in this subject in two organizations which did much work in investigating the authenticity of the inscription. One was the Minnesota Historical Society; the other was The Norwegian Society, a cultural club in Minneapolis.

During the year 1908, I was fully occupied in completing the manuscript of my book on the Norwegian immigration, and I did little traveling that year. But in the spring of 1909 I made my second trip to Kensington. My purpose was to learn what I could about Mr. Ohman's reputation and also to learn if he was a skilled stonecutter. Many times during the winter I had admired the fine cutting of the runic letters in the inscription which seemed to be the work of an artist with a cold-chisel.

As practically everyone in or near Kensington had seen the inscription and knew the Olof Ohman family well, it was easy to make inquiries, but not once was any suspicion against him mentioned. He was evidently respected as a useful citizen who somehow managed to make a living on a tract of land which all the early settlers had thought was worthless. The last man I talked with was the local pastor who said he had only recently been stationed there and knew little about the local people. As he followed me to the door, he asked me if I had heard about the Swedish grammar which contained a runic alphabet. I told him no and asked him to explain.

He did not know much about it, he said. There had been an unfrocked Swedish minister named Sven Fogelblad, he told me, who occasionally visited friends in the neighborhood. When Fogelblad died, a Swedish grammar containing a runic alphabet had been found with a few other books among his possessions. It is said that Ohman later borrowed this grammar to help him decipher the inscription.

This was important news. The finder of the stone had or had had a book containing runes! I hurried to Ohman's house. He was not at home, but his wife recognized me from my previous visit and invited me in. I wasted no time in making my inquiry. I said: "Mrs. Ohman, do you have a book that your husband bought or borrowed from Mr. Fogelblad?"

"Do you mean that Swedish grammar? Here it is."

She reached up to a shelf where a couple of books were lying and took down one of them. Yes, there it was, C. J L. *Almquist, Svensk Grammatik*, 1840. Quickly I turned to the page containing the runes. They were the standard runes of the tenth and eleventh centuries when runic writing was widely used, but the alphabet of the Kensington inscription had many that were different. Moreover, the grammar contained no runic numerals, while the stone had eight. The author of the inscription could obviously not have obtained his runes from the grammar.

It was time to go, and as I picked up my hat, I asked: "Does Mr. Ohman have much mason work?"

"Mason work? He is not a mason. He does some carpenter work when he has time." I told her I had been misinformed and bid her goodby.

Some time later I was in St. Paul and mentioned this

grammar to Professor N. H. Winchell, the state archaeologist. I added that I did not think it gave any clue to the origin of the inscription. However, Winchell was much impressed. He immediately went up to Kensington and bought the book from Ohman. As Winchell could not read Swedish, he asked J. A. Holvik, a former student at the University of Oslo, to make a study of the grammar to see if it had any connection with the inscription on the stone. Holvik was a disbeliever in the authenticity of the inscription, but he gave the grammar a careful study. He then wrote a report of about five hundred words, ending with the conclusion that "it is evident that there is no connection between the inscription on the Kensington Stone and the book bearing the name Sv. Fogelblad."[2]

Before I left Kensington, I made inquiries about Sven Fogelblad. This carried me to several other counties in the state. The report on him was therefore not completed on this visit but a year or so later. Here are briefly the main facts of what is known about him.

He was born in 1829, studied theology at the University of Uppsala, and about 1860 was a curate under Rev. Rolander in Tomberg parish, West Gothland. Nothing is known about his length of service as a Lutheran pastor, but as he was too much given to drink, he was finally defrocked. He emigrated to Litchfield, Minnesota, at the end of the Indian War (1865), and, as the pioneers were greatly in need of a minister, he here had a chance to rehabilitate himself. But again, his old trouble tripped him up. He came to his first service drunk.

This was Fogelblad's last chance as a pastor, and he became a sort of a gentleman tramp. However, he paid his way in a certain fashion by becoming a teacher of religion in people's homes. In this way he won strong support among the mothers in many settlements because they did not want their children to grow up ignorant of the fundamental teachings of their faith. Moreover, he was always welcome after an absence of many months because he brought news of the births, weddings and deaths of friends in other settlements. He was the forerunner of the village newspapers.

He came to the vicinity of Kensington some time in the 1880's and I spoke with many men who knew him well and liked him. They all said that any idea that he had chiseled the runestone was entirely unthinkable. He was too lazy for anything requiring toil and knew nothing about handling tools such as a stonecutter's chisel, a carpenter's saw, or even a farmer's hay fork. Moreover, he was not interested in history and read very little.[3]

chapter five

THE ROUTE OF THE EXPEDITION

The location of the discovery of the Kensington Stone quite understandably placed its authenticity under doubt from the start. How could a small party of medieval northmen have penetrated so far inland, and for what purpose?

Actually, western Minnesota was not so difficult of access from the Atlantic seaboard in medieval times as might be supposed. A series of rivers and lakes leads right up to the spot where the Minnesota runestone was found. But that is not enough. *Why* did they push so far north and west?

To learn the purpose of the long trek we must go back to King Magnus' letter to the commandant in which the purpose of the expedition is explicitly stated. This purpose was to restore Christianity in Greenland. The king says:

> *We do this for the honor of God, and for the sake of our soul, and for the sake of our predecessors, who in Greenland established Christianity and have maintained it until this time, and we will not let it perish in our day.*

The only place in Greenland where Christianity was threatened was in the Western colony. There it was more than threatened; it was even reported that the people in that settlement had given up the true faith and gone to live with the heathen people of Vinland. To fulfill the king's instructions it would be necessary to seek these people wherever they had gone and restore them to the Church, because the king said his own salvation depended upon it.

As this search might take several years, the first thing to do would be to establish a headquarters in a good harbor where a fortified base of operations could be built and food grown while the search for the Greenlanders proceeded. This headquarters is implied in the inscription which says that this exploring party came from Vinland, not Norway.

Briefly, the timetable of the expedition can be hypothicated as follows: The king's written order authorizing the expedition is dated about November 1, 1354.[1] It is doubtful if it would be ready to sail the next spring. In any event it did not sail in 1355 which was so stormy in the north that, according to the Icelandic annals for that year, no ships ventured out. It therefore did not depart until 1356, and as the harbors of Greenland are jammed with ice until August, it could not make a landing in Greenland until sometime in that month.

There was probably a stay of some days in the Eastern Settlement to learn if anything was known of the exiles and also to procure fresh food and water. Undoubtedly a trip would be made to the Western Settlement to examine conditions there and to see if the emigrants possibly had returned to their old homes. These delays would make it unwise to proceed to Vinland so late in that fall of 1356.

On arriving in Vinland and selecting a good harbor in the fall of 1357, the first logical thing would be to establish a fortified base. There is reason to believe this was at Rhode Island. No progress in searching for the lost people could be made until the base was built.

In the king's letter to Sir Paul, he orders that the "Knorr," the royal freight vessel, be used in this voyage. But this heavy ship was of too big draught to be used in the shallow waters near the shore while searching for signs of the Greenlanders. Light vessels of shallow draught would also be needed. The Kensington inscription implies that there were at least two because it says that ten men were left to look after the ships.[2]

With thirty men in two light ships, it would be possible in 1358 to search the shore from Rhode Island to the north end of Nova Scotia. In 1359 the islands to the north and Newfoundland could perhaps be covered; and in 1360 the St. Lawrence basin and part of the coast of Labrador could be examined, perhaps as far north as Hamilton Inlet. All these shores may have seemed promising.

North of Hamilton Inlet the coast soon becomes treeless and mountainous, and their expectation of finding the emigrants must have faded. However, there was one possibility that would urge them on. They knew nothing about the geography of America, but they may have assumed that it was a big island like Greenland. They knew that Greenland's east coast was unfit for human habitation, but its west coast was tolerable. This would suggest the possibility that the west coast of this new land that they were passing might also be habitable, like the west coast of Greenland, and such a possibility would urge them on.

When they finally came to the end of the Ungava Peninsula and reached Hudson Bay, the situation looked more promising, for here the coast runs straight south for nine hundred miles. Hopefully they would look for green meadows like those in Greenland. But the east coast of Hudson Bay is a high, rocky land of desolation. It would now be getting late in the season, and their main need would be to find a safe harbor and a suitable place for a winter camp with plenty of timber for fuel. These two requisites they would hardly find until they reached the mouth of the Nelson River, perhaps in the fall of 1361.

It must now have been clear to them that the search for the apostate Greenlanders was hopeless. Twenty years had passed since the Greenlanders had disappeared, and they must have perished. It now remained for them to return to Vinland and sail back to Norway on the other side of Atlantic. Here the question probably arose: Which way shall we go? Shall we return the way we came, past thousands of miles of bleak mountains, or shall we try an overland route by help of the rivers? An overland route might well be shorter.

That supposition, if made, was quite right. They had circumnavigated two sides of a great quadrangle and half of the third side, so the overland route would be shorter. In addition to this there might well have been another, and possibly even stronger, urge to see what the inside of this vast land looked like. Was it a desert wilderness, or was it a new world of strange sights and treasures like the marvelous China whose wonders had just recently been revealed by the great traveler, Marco Polo? To the intelligent, capable young men of this group, made up of men of the king's bodyguard and other men of superior mettle, this chance to explore a new country must have been alluring. Whatever their motivation, the party divided in the late spring or early summer of 1362. Prudence would prompt the travelers to leave their vessels guarded in case an overland return to Vinland was not found possible. The inscription says that ten men were left to take care of the ships while twenty men went inland. It also tells what happened to the twenty men; in another chapter I shall present evidence showing that two of these ten men were lost, but the surviving eight returned to Greenland in 1363 and to Bergen in 1363 or 1364.

Wahlgren thinks that this venture of the twenty men into the interior was an idiotic performance. He quotes Dr. Roberto Almagio, president of the Academy of Rome, to prove it:

> "An expedition of this nature, the purpose of which, furthermore, is not apparent, if carried out in the manner supposed by Holand, could be conceived of only if it had been preceded and prepared by a long series of more limited but repeated reconnaissances towards the interior, concerning which there it not the slightest evidence." In other words, Almagio very reasonably assumes that men of the caliber we must suppose for the purpose of a royal expedition would behave like canny, trained explorers rather than like wandering nomads or a pack of fools, clutching at every straw in order to execute a purpose, or shifting series of purposes which have no demonstrable reality outsides of Mr. Holand's imagination. Concerning this last point, nothing is so illuminating as a reading, in sequence, of Holand's own self-contradictory suppositions as they have developed, decade by decade. Carefully read, Holand is the best refutation of Holand.[3]

It is apparent that Dr. Almagio is thinking of a modern scientific expedition with plenty of funds. But most of the explorations in America (and we have had scores of them) were of the old-fashioned kind which were not "preceded and prepared by a long series of reconnaissances." One of the first was

Jean Nicolet's voyage from the lower St. Lawrence to the head
of Green Bay in Wisconsin in 1634. Another great exploratory
voyage was Louis Jolliet's and Jacques Marquette's voyage from
Mackinac Island to the mouth of the Arkansas River, a distance,
going and coming, of about four thousand miles. Two white
men and five Indians in two birchbark canoes made that journey
in four months.

The most important of these explorations and most like the
one mentioned on the Kensington Stone was the Lewis and
Clark expedition from St. Louis to the Pacific and back in
1804-6. It started out with forty-five men on May 14 and proceeded by boats up the Missouri River, arriving at a village of the
Mandans, north of the site of Bismarck, North Dakota, late in
October, a distance of 1600 miles. Here they sent fourteen men
back to St. Louis; they spent the winter with the Mandans.

On April 7, they resumed their journey with about thirty
men, and after having traversed a thousand miles of mountainous
area, they reached the Pacific, November 7, the same year, 1805.
In that year they covered 2,650 miles, mostly upstream. In 1806
they started on their return trip March 23 and reached St. Louis
on September 23, a distance of 4,250 miles. I think Dr. Almagio
will agree that this was a very great expedition even if it was
not preceded and prepared "by a long series of more limited but
repeated reconnaissances toward the interior."

But Wahlgren has other objections. There is, worst of all,
the problem of ascending "the tempestuous Nelson." He quotes
another critic of the Kensington inscription, Dr. Milo Quaife:

> We may now consider the problems involved in the
> ascent, by the explorers, of the Nelson River. The very
> roadstead where the vessel must lie for a year is one of the
> most dangerous places for shipping in the world. Into the
> trumpet-like river mouth, seven miles wide at its outer
> extremity, sweeps a twelve-foot tide, bearing two-thirds of
> the year the ice masses of Hudson Bay. The river itself is
> commonly ice-locked until July, and the period when boats
> may proceed from York Factory to the interior is limited
> to three months. . . . Lake Winnipeg, fifth in size in
> America, assembles the rainfall of almost half-a-million

square miles of country, and by the Nelson River discharges
into Hudson Bay. The mighty flood, ranging from 50,000 to
150,000 cubic feet a second, makes the seven-hundred-foot
descent from the lake to the bay in a series of chutes and
rapids, interspersed with stretches of level water or lakes.
The current divides and redivides; while the lakes are
plentifully bestrewn with islands to bewilder the explorer.
Although the ascent of the river may be physically possible,
so arduous and dangerous is the task that not even the
natives will undertake it, and in almost two hundred years of
occupancy of the region by the Hudson Bay Company,
with constant necessity of travel between York Factory and
the interior, there seems to be no single record of any ascent
of the Nelson River by trader or explorer.[4]

The above quotation is filled with errors.[5] There is in
Madison, Wisconsin, a lawyer named T. H. Field who has been
to Hudson Bay several times. I asked him if the above description
of Nelson River was correct. In a letter of November 20, 1947,
he replies as follows:

Quaife's statement about travel on the Nelson is ridiculous
and shows lack of knowledge about river travel in general
and particularly the rivers in Canada. I have travelled to
Hudson Bay three times, and each time used river travel,
and there is nothing difficult about it.

In a letter written October 20, 1941, Mr. Field writes:

In the summer of 1941 my wife and I secured a twenty-
foot Hudson Bay freight canoe at Norway House and took
with us a native guide and descended the Nelson River.
We were not experienced canoe men, but had no difficulty.
The canoe that we used was similar to what the Hudson
Bay Company now use for freighting to their inland posts.
It was made of birch ribs with light spruce planking
covered with canvas, and the carrying capacity of a 20-foot
canoe is one ton. The ascent of the river is in many ways
easier than descending because it is possible to pole the
boat through the rapids and you do not have the danger
of striking submerged rocks, as you do in descending the

stream. We took plenty of time, loafed, fished, went hunting, and had a grand three weeks' vacation. We returned by rail while the guide made the trip up the river in less than three weeks. I had pointed out to me a York boat at the portages, and I could see the scratch marks still on the rocks from the York boats.

I also have a letter from Olaf Olson, Spring Valley, New York, in which he says he has a copy of a letter from his uncle, Carl Martin Olson, who was stationed at Fort York at the mouth of the Nelson River. "On September 2, 1860, he left Fort York and arrived at the Upper Fort Garry (now in the city of Winnipeg) on September 26. His trip was twice as far as to Norway House and was achieved in three and a half weeks"—more evidence that Quaife greatly overrates its hazards.

So much for what Wahlgren calls "the insane and fruitless project of ascending the Nelson." Quoting Quaife, Wahlgren says:

> . . . the very roadstead where the vessel must lie for a year is one of the most dangerous places for shipping in the world. Into the trumpet-like river mouth, seven miles wide at its outer extremity, sweeps a twelve-foot tide, bearing during two-thirds of the year the ice masses of Hudson Bay.

But there is nothing to compel a ship to lie in that open roadstead for a year. The river is broad and deep up to Seal Island, twenty-five miles up the river, which is as far as the tide reaches. And the Northmen were accustomed to pull their ships up on land for the winter.

The inscription says that the travelers left ten men in charge of the ships, "14 day-voyage" from the finding place of the stone. This description of the distance from the sea has evoked much doubt of the authenticity of the inscription. Obviously many weeks and possibly months would have been required to reach Minnesota. Some commentators, like Wahlgren, have been most sarcastic in referring to it. What they apparently do not know is that all Norse and English authorities such as Nansen, Gathorne-Hardy, Wm. Hovgaard and Fossum agree that the term day's sail or day voyage was a unit of distance equal to about 75 English miles.[6] There is no reason for supposing that they would abandon this term for some other. Being accustomed to dead reckoning, they would have no great difficulty in adding each day's progress to make a "day-voyage," just as Lewis and Clark added up their daily distances on their voyage. The distance from the finding place of the stone to the sea would therefore be 14 times 75, or 1050 miles. According to the *New International Encyclopedia,* the distance from the sea at tidewater to the outlet of Lake Winnipeg is "about 400 miles." The distance from the north end of Lake Winnipeg to the city of Winnipeg is also 400 miles. From Winnipeg to Kensington is about 300 miles, which makes a total of 1080 to 1100 miles from the mouth of the Nelson to the finding place of the stone.

Thus we see that, given the purpose of the expedition, it could very well have arrived in western Minnesota, unless the lost Greenlanders were found, or the expedition came to an end, before arriving there. Their search for the apostates would necessitate their following the Atlantic shore northward, which would lead them into Hudson Bay. Their curiosity, together with their hope of returning to the headquarters, would prompt them to seek a river leading southward. As their headquarters lay far to the east they would shun any river leading westward. Thus they would reach and follow the Red River to its southeastern headwaters where their inscription was found.

chapter six

THE SIZE AND AGE OF THE
TREE ABOVE THE STONE

In the summer of 1909, I was invited by Dr. Knut Hoegh, a prominent surgeon in Minneapolis, to accompany him on a trip to Kensington to learn the circumstances of the discovery of the stone. As the Doctor said, "there may be more than one version." In Minneapolis he was the president of a cultural society, known as the Norwegian Society, and he had been requested to act as chairman of a committee to investigate the circumstances of the find. There had been many guesses about the age of the tree. I had been told by someone that the tree was twenty-five years old "as shown by the annual rings of growth," and this I had put into my early report. Later, Olof Ohman wrote me that no tree rings had been counted. It was therefore necessary to make a thorough inquiry into the age of the tree.

We went to the Kensington neighborhood and interviewed a dozen men, each one separately in his own home. There was only one version. These men had all seen the tree under which the stone was found and had inspected the two main roots, which held the stone in a rigid clasp and were flat where they had been in contact with the stone.

As we had no need of so many statements, we selected five. Of these, two were by Olof Ohman and his son because they had found the stone; the third was by Nils Flaten, the nearest neighbor, who was present when the stone was found. The fourth was by Samuel Olson, a jeweler and optician in Kensington. He seemed to have the best education of the men with

whom we talked. The fifth was by Roald Bentson, a farmer
whom Dr. Hoegh knew well from the time he had practiced
medicine in La Crosse. He lived about a mile away and had
seen the stone a day or two after it was found. Hoegh called
him a fine representative of a dependable and intelligent
Norwegian farmer.[1]

These men were asked if they would write out what they
had told us and go before a notary public and swear to the
truth of it. All were willing to make the affidavit, but three of
them asked us to write it out for them as they were not familiar
with the process of expressing themselves in writing. We did so
and read their statements to them, and they were satisfied as to
the correctness of the written statements. These three were Olof
Ohman, his son Edward, and Nils Flaten. The other two,
Roald Bentson and Samuel Olson, preferred to write their own
statements. The following is the statement written by Olof
Ohman; then follows the joint statement of Roald Bentson and
Samuel Olson:

I, Olof Ohman, of the town of Solem, Douglas County,
State of Minnesota, being duly sworn, make the following
statement:

I am fifty-four years of age, and was born in Helsingland,
Sweden, from where I emigrated to America in the year
1881, and settled upon my farm in Section Fourteen, township of Solem, in 1891. In the month of August, 1898,
while accompanied by my son, Edward, I was engaged in
grubbing upon a timbered elevation, surrounded by marshes,
in the south-east corner of my land, about 500 feet west of
my neighbor's, Nils Flaten's, house, and in the full view
thereof. Upon removing an asp, measuring about 10 inches
in diameter at its base, I discovered a flat stone inscribed
with characters, to me unintelligible. The stone lay just
beneath the surface of the ground in a slightly slanting
position, with one corner almost protruding. The two
largest roots of the tree clasped the stone in such a manner
that the stone must have been there at least as long as the
tree. One of the roots penetrated directly downward and
was flat on the side next to the stone. The other root
extended almost horizontally across the stone and made at

its edge a right-angled turn downward. At this turn the root was flattened on the side toward the stone. This root was about three inches in diameter. Upon washing off the surface dirt, the inscription presented a weathered appearance, which to me appeared just as old as the untouched parts of the stone. I immediately called my neighbor's, Nils Flaten's, attention to the discovery, and he came over the same afternoon and inspected the stone and the stump under which it was found.

I kept the stone in my possession for a few days; and then left it in the Bank of Kensington, where it remained for inspection for several months. During this interval, it was sent to Chicago for inspection and soon returned in the same state in which it was sent. Since then I kept it at my farm until August, 1907, when I presented the stone to H. R. Holand. The stone, as I remember, was about 30 inches long, 16 inches wide, and 7 inches thick, and I recognize the illustration on page 16 of H. R. Holand's History of Norwegian Settlements of America, as being a photographic reproduction of the stone's inscription.

(Signed)   Olof Ohman.

Witness:
R. J. Rasmusson
George H. Merhes

State of Minnesota,
County of Douglas

On this 20th day of July, 1909, personally came before me, a Notary Public in and for Douglas County and State of Minnesota, Mr. Olof Ohman, to me known to be the described in the foregoing document, and acknowledged that he executed the same as his free act and deed.

(Signed)   R. J. Rasmusson
(Seal)   Notary Public,
Douglas County, Minnesota

My commission expires November 17, 1915.

Bentson's and Olson's joint statement reads thus:

We, the undersigned, residents of Kensington, Minn., and vicinity, hereby testify to the fact that we have seen a stone with an inscription in characters to us unintelligible, of which it was alleged, and which we truthfully believe, was discovered and dug out of the ground in August, 1898, about four miles N.E. of Kensington, Minn., on the S.E. corner of the S.W. ¼ of the N.E. ¼ of Section 14, Town 127, Range 40 W., by one Olof Ohman and his son Edward Ohman. We further testify that we saw the hole in the ground in which it was stated that the stone had been imbedded. The inscription as seen by us presented an ancient and weathered appearance, similar to the uninscribed parts of the stone. We saw the root of an asp that was eight inches to ten inches in diameter at the bottom of the trunk, of which it was alleged that it had grown on one side of the stone, and in close contact with same. We saw the stump of this tree, and are convinced that it had been in close contact with the stone because of its peculiar shape. One of the roots that had pursued a perpendicular course downward was flattened on one side, as we think because of its contact with the stone.

We saw another root of the same stump about three inches in diameter which had taken an almost horizontal course from the body of the stump. About eighteen inches from its junction with the first mentioned root, this second root made a right-angled bend and continued downward. It was flattened and expanded on its interior bend. We are convinced that the two roots above described exactly conformed to the configuration of the stone. The stone was about thirty inches long, sixteen inches wide and seven inches thick. We recognize the illustration on page 16 of H. R. Holand's History of the Norwegian Settlements as being a photographic reproduction of the inscription on the face of the stone.

(Signed)   Roald Bentson
            S. Olson

Witness:
  R. J. Rasmusson
  George H. Merhes

State of Minnesota
County of Douglas

On this 20th day of July, 1909, personally came before me, a Notary Public in and for Douglas County and State of Minnesota, Mr. Roald Bentson and Mr. S. Olson, to me known to be the persons described in the foregoing document, and acknowledged that they executed the same as their free act and deed.

(Signed)   R. J. Rasmusson
(Seal)   Notary Public,
Douglas County, Minnesota

My commission expires November 17, 1915.

All four affidavits are printed in my first book on this subject, *The Kensington Stone*, 1932, pp. 34-37, 292-95.

Likewise, the early reports in the newspapers a few weeks after the stone was found give the same details about the encircling roots with their 90° angles. There is a very clear report on the discovery by Olaus Olson of Holmes City, written a few months after the stone was found.[2] He describes the roots in much detail. He was a member of a company of men from Alexandria, led by the County Superintendent of Schools, C. W. Van Dyke, who came to inspect the finding place, all of whom, he reports, were satisfied that the stone was in its finding place before the tree began to grow.

Ten years later Professor N.H. Winchell heard of the visit of this large party, and he wrote to nine of them asking them to describe the stump of the tree. Their replies were all to the effect that "the roots of the tree, especially the largest one which ran across the surface of the stone, were flattened by contact with the stone."[3]

Dr. Hoegh was now called back to his patients, and we returned to Minneapolis well satisfied. We had learned beyond any reasonable doubt the approximate size of the tree above the stone, the appearance of the inscription, and the fact that the roots which held the stone were flat where they had come in contact with the stone. This showed conclusively that the stone had been in its finding place at least as long as the tree had stood there. It now remained to determine the approximate age of the tree.

In the summer of 1910, we were again in the Kensington neighborhood. We asked Mr. Ohman to cut down a couple of trees of the same size as described in his affidavit so we could get a cross section of the trunks and count the annual rings of growth. He was unable to find any of the right size on the hill where the stone was found, but finally found two down in a hollow where the soil was moist and rich; but he objected that these trees were healthy and did not correctly represent the tree under which the stone was found because that tree was sickly and stunted. (This was verified by Professor Flom who, the following year, spent some days there interviewing the early settlers).[4] In lieu of anything better, these two trees were cut down and a cross section of each was marked A and B. Later, Ohman found a stunted tree which in its growth resembled "the runestone tree." A cross section of this was also cut and marked C.

These cross sections were given to N. H. Winchell, the state archaeologist, who had them dried and varnished. When this was done, the annual growth rings appeared distinctly and showed the following number: A, 37 rings; B, 42; and C, 38. At least five years must be added to each for the decayed and blurred center, the rings of which could not be counted. These cross sections are now in the possession of the Minnesota Historical Society.[5]

We now had five estimates on the size of the tree in question, ranging from 8½ to 10 inches in diameter.[6] The mean average of these five estimates is 9.2 inches at the stump. As C with a diameter of 5.5 inches at the stump was 43 years old, a tree of this kind of growth having a diameter of 9.2 would be 72 years old, if, as stated by Ohman, the tree had a stunted growth.

But Dr. Hoegh was cautious. "What if Ohman is wrong about the tree above the stone being sickly? It is safer, I think, to assume that it was a healthy tree. Then we will be sure that our estimates are safe."

The minimum age of the tree is therefore 42 years. This

brings us back to 1856 which was 25 years before Ohman came to America and 11 years before the first pioneers came to Kensington or any part of Douglas county.

The testimony on the age of the tree is so complete and convincing that very few people will find fault with it.[7] Wahlgren, however, is suspicious that nothing is said about the *height* of the tree. Thus he says: "The conspicuous omission from Mr. Holand's elaborate structure of speculation of any mention of the *height* of the tree is a cause for wonder. Was the height of the tree really a matter of indifference?"

Of course it was, because nothing can be learned of the age of a tree by its height. This depends largely on the density of the surrounding timber. If this is thick, the tree will be much taller and slimmer than a tree of the same age growing in the open, where its growth will spread sidewise. Wahlgren declares that this omission of all mention of the height of the tree was "due to the discovery of facts, inconvenient facts . . . which its protagonists have not deemed it necessary to produce for scholarly assessments."[8]

In the next paragraph he goes even farther astray: He says "at all events, *the Kensington tree was never to our certain knowledge seen by anybody*. Cut from its stump at a point from 12 to 18 inches above its roots, it was speedily removed from the runesite, one must suppose, and converted into firewood before questions could be asked."

A few pages later, however, he quotes part of a letter to Winchell, written by C. W. Van Dyke, County Superintendent of Schools, who was a member of the party of nine men from Alexandria who visited the finding place of the stone in the spring of 1899. In this letter Van Dyke says: "The tree, as indicated by its roots, had undoubtedly grown over some flat stone."[9] He adds that he inspected the tree but unfortunately did not cut a cross section off its base which would have shown the age of the tree.

Wahlgren cites the discrepancy in various accounts as to the month when the stone was found, the four affidavits giving it as August, the letter by Olaus Olson citing November and suggests that this disagreement indicates duplicity on somebody's part.[10]

It does not occur to Wahlgren that this uncertainty as to the month of the year is a simple case of forgetfulness. How many men or women can recall the date of an event outside of family life ten or twelve years ago? There is no reason why anyone should remember the month when the stone was found. The fact that an inscribed stone was found was locally of considerable interest, but as the inscription, as then read, did not make good sense and was rejected as a fake by those who were supposed to know, this greatly chilled the interest and people turned their thoughts to other things.

Wahlgren also makes much of the fact that Ohman and Flaten state in their affidavits that the house of the latter was five hundred feet from the finding place of the stone, whereas is was actually more than 1,200 feet. The mistake was presumably due to the very common tendency of underestimating distances in well-known areas.

Professor Wahlgren is naturally must concerned about the affidavits because if they are what they claim to be, the inscribed stone was in its finding place at least forty-two years before it was found in 1898, and Wahlgren's claim is shattered. To begin with, he points out that I in my later writings sometimes give all the credit to Dr. Hoegh and sometimes claim that I was present. Perhaps this is true. Dr. Hoegh was the leader in this affair and planned the procedure. I admired him very much for his tact, his intelligence and kindness, and that prompted even a selfish person like me to give him all the credit. At other times I said we worked together, which is true.

But Wahlgren doubts that these affidavits ever existed. He asks: "Are there, or have there ever been, any affidavits?" "Did Dr. Hoegh or Mr. Holand really secure the originals of these affidavits?" "Why could Dr. Hoegh speak of only one affidavit—Bentson's—in the fall of 1909?" "Has anyone ever seen the original affidavits?"

The answers to these questions are as follows: In the *Journal of American History* for 1910, Volume IV, page 178, the Olof

Ohman affidavit is printed in full, and a comparison of it with the text in my book, *The Kensington Stone*, 1932, pages 34 and 35, will show that it is word for word the same.

In a letter to Dr. Upham, December 12, 1909, which is preserved in the Minnesota historical archives, I say: "Enclosed I send you copies of the other three affidavits." These are the affidavits of Edward Ohman, Nils Flaten, and the joint affidavit of Roald and S. Olson.

Dr. Hoegh in his report to the Norwegian Society mentions Roald Bentson, a former neighbor and patient of his, for whom he had the highest regard. He says: "All the neighbors had full faith in Olof Ohman, among them Roald Bentson, an old pioneer, well known in Kensington, a complete type of a dependable, intelligent, Norwegian farmer. He is convinced of the truth of the find concerning the roots (of the tree) also that there had been no digging there previously, concerning which he has given sworn testimony. Many others are willing to and have to me confirmed the same as Bentson."[12]

Thus we see that copies of all the four affidavits were sent to the Minnesota Historical Society. Then they were published in New York, Minneapolis and Decorah as early as 1909 and 1910—all precise copies of the originals which I retained. Unfortunately, in June, 1934, my house was struck by lightning, and all my books and papers were destroyed by fire. But Wahlgren is not yet through with the affidavits. He admits that R. J. Rasmusson, the Notary Public who administered the oath to the signers of the affidavits had been properly appointed on November 17, 1908; but his certificate of notaryship was not recorded until late in 1910. Wahlgren therefore thinks that these affidavits "have no standing as legal documents." This seems hardly tenable. Rasmusson had been properly appointed, and the neglect of a careless clerk would not invalidate his notaryship.

The next year after Dr. Hoegh and I made our investigation of the age of the tree, Professor Flom spent five days in the same neighborhood making his own investigation of the circumstances of the find. In his lecture before the Illinois Historical Society in 1910, he comments on our investigation as follows:

The basis of the discussion has been the conditions surrounding the discovery of the stone, there being apparently no evidence of fraud here. Among these are the fact that the stone was actually found in the ground. The veracity of the men who saw the stone and the tree, the apparent age of the tree, the weathering of the stone, the recent settlement of that locality, the unlikelihood that any of the early settlers of that region should have possessed the knowledge of runes, or if so had any reason for foisting such a fraud upon the public.[13]

Meanwhile the Museum Committee of the Minnesota Historical Society was making its own investigation. It consisted of the following members: E. C. Mitchell, Antiquarian, Chairman; F. J. Schaefer, Historian and Rector St. Paul Seminary; O. D. Wheeler, Archeologist and Attorney; N. H. Winchell, Geologist and State Archeologist; Warren Upham, Geologist and Secretary of the Society. These men were all strangers to me, and I knew nothing about their attitude, with one exception, until the report of their investigation was made. The exception was Professor N. H. Winchell who told me that when the committee began its work, he had no faith in the inscription or in me. However, as the work proceeded, he became its best defender. Being a group of middle-aged scholarly men, they were well qualified to sit as a jury to consider the arguments pro and con on the authenticity of the inscription. As the well-known Msgr. Rev. J. M. Reardon says about this committee: "All were recognized scholars capable of judging the value and force of linguistic arguments and weighing judicially the evidence adduced. In this investigation they had the help of American and European experts in runology and Scandinavian literature."[14]

Eventually after more than a year of investigation and discussion, the committee agreed upon a report favoring the authenticity of the inscription, and all its members signed it, making no reservations. This was presented and discussed at the monthly meeting of the Executive Council held May 9, 1910. The council then ordered that it be received and printed with the statement that "the Council and the Society reserve their conclusion until more agreement of opinions for or against the rune inscription may be attained."[15]

At the time (in 1910) when the committee presented its first report, it knew nothing about the Paul Knutson expedition, which is one of the best evidences of the authenticity of the inscription. It continued its hearings and discussions for two or three years more, whereupon it again published its unanimous conclusion that the inscription was authentic.

Mr. Wahlgren suggests and asserts that I practically wrote the report of the committee. This is absurd. No one could dictate to these men. I did not attend any of the committee's meetings, nor did I contribute anything to their deliberations except when asked, which was seldom. I had previously published some articles on the inscription and these were accessible to the committee; but so also were papers against the inscription written by H. Gjessing, O. J. Breda, R. B. Anderson, G. Bothne and others; and George Flom and C. N. Gould were sending opposing arguments almost every week. As the committee found better evidence in the contributions of those who defended the stone than in Flom's or Gould's arguments, Wahlgren concludes that the committee was incompetent.

Wahlgren finds it highly suspicious that I have not discussed the whetstone which was reported to have been found by men digging in the spot where the tree had stood in the hope of finding a grave or a treasure. Ohman said it was not like modern whetstones and it broke in two and was dropped in the hole. I have not seen it nor do I see how this whetstone proves anything because whetstones have been in use for thousands of years. Now Wahlgren claims it was modern, and that I said nothing about it because it was "practically an important clue to the commission of a hoax."[17]

One would think that such a thorough investigation backed with sworn statements and checked and approved by the MHS Committee would be accepted by all intelligent men, but not so. After reviewing it all, Wahlgren comes out with the amazing statement that "There is no reason for assuming that the Kensington carving antedates the year 1898."[18] With this preposterous statement he attempts to brush aside all evidence which is contrary to his personal theory. This is "scientific research" with a vengeance!

On page 58 Wahlgren adds the following schoolmasterly remarks:

> It should be clearly understood that the authenticity of a questioned artifact is not the sort of thing that can be established through affidavits, however phrased or attested. Only science can give the answer through the application of research methods that have won general acceptance in the branches of science concerned.

Mr. Wahlgren forgets that the men who signed these affidavits were not attempting to solve any scientific problem. They were merely reporting on the size of a certain tree and the appearance of its roots. Then Wahlgren adds the following false accusation (page 58):

> If the contradictory and very late affidavits of Olof Ohman and Nils Flaten are to be taken seriously, they show at worst, that two men voluntarily committed a legal fraud or were somehow persuaded to execute the documents contrary to their own inclination; or, at best, that Ohman and Flaten were personally innocent of complicity in a hoax. In no other way do the affidavits authenticate the rune stone itself.

In what respects are these two affidavits contradictory? Ohman says:

> The stone lay just beneath the surface of the ground in a slightly slanting position, with one corner almost protruding. The two largest roots of the tree clasped the stone in such a manner that the stone must have been there at least as long as the tree. One of the roots penetrated directly downward and was flat on the side next to the stone. The other extended almost horizontally across the stone and made at its edge a right angled turn downward. At this turn the root was flattened on the side toward the stone. This root was about three inches in diameter.

The following is Flaten's description:

> I . . . saw a stone about 30 inches long, 16 inches wide
> and 6 inches thick, which was covered with strange
> characters upon two sides and for more than half its length.
> The inscription presented a very ancient and weathered
> appearance. Mr. Ohman showed me an asp tree about 8 to
> 10 inches in diameter at its base, beneath which, he alleged,
> the stone was found. The two largest roots of the asp were
> flattened on their inner surface and bent by nature in such
> a way as to exactly conform to the outlines of the stone.
> I inspected this hole and can testify to the fact that the
> stone had been there prior to the growth of the tree, as
> the spot was in close proximity to my house.

I see nothing contradictory in these two statements. Why
then intimate that these men were rogues and liars?

Dr. Hoegh was a man of broad culture as well as a competent surgeon. He was also much interested in psychology. On
the two visits I made with him to Kensington, he spent much
time with Olof Ohman, against whom there was then some
suspicion—not locally, but in the newspapers—that he had
inscribed the stone. On our second return to Minneapolis, he
said he was convinced that there was not the least possibility
that Ohman, aside from finding the stone, had anything to do
with it. This he also affirms in his committee report. He wrote:

> There is no possibility that Ohman could have fabricated
> the inscription. He is an intelligent but unschooled rustic
> who, according to his own statement, had only a few months'
> schooling in all his life. He gives the impression of being a
> very reliable man; his personality would make him an
> excellent witness in a court trial. . . . His conduct after he
> found the stone is just what it should be if the find was
> authentic.
>
> Olof Ohman cannot with the least reasonableness be
> assumed to have cut the runes, planted the stone or dug it
> up again.[19]

Professor Winchell, who also had spent much time with
Ohman, testifies to Ohman's frankness and dependability. He
writes:

The honesty and candor of Mr. Olof Ohman become evident to anyone who converses with him. . . . Not one of all who have interviewed Mr. Ohman, whether believers or non-believers in the authenticity of the inscription has seen any reason to question his veracity.[20]

Professor Wahlgren is an ingenious opponent. If he does not find the evidence he needs, he is not daunted. This is illustrated on page 41 of his book. He says:

Professor Winchell reported at the meeting of the MHS on December 13, 1909, that it was Flaten who had uncovered the stone and found no writing on it, after which the stone lay neglected for a long time.

This would be most important evidence if true, and I wrote to Dr. Russell W. Fridley, Director of the Society, and asked him for a copy of the statement attributed to Professor Winchell. The following is Dr. Fridley's reply, dated April 20, 1960:

We have checked the original minutes and do not find the statement quoted on page 41 of Professor Wahlgren's book. The only statement quoted on this matter by Professor Winchell recorded in the minutes is as follows: "Professor N. H. Winchell spoke of the stone as from a large drift boulder and of his identification of 'two skerries' . . ."

Mr. Frederick J. Pohl has called attention to a similar gratuitous invention by Wahlgren. Pohl writes:

In his index, p. 223, Wahlgren has this entry: "AVM: in Rosander, 137." It is undeniable that the three capital letters A, V, and M do appear on pages of Rosander, but unfortunately for Professor Wahlgren, they never appear consecutively in that order. The expression A V M is not in Rosander. . . . Wahlgren cannot evade responsibility for the misleading statement that A V M is in Rosander; and all the more so since he forces the misconception on the unwary in his own referred-to page 137, where after quoting the phrase *AVM fraelse af illu* from the Kensington inscription, he pushes his argument to an unjustifiable conclusion: *"Comparing the phrase found on the Kensington Stone with the parallel in Rosander, it is obvious that we need look no further."*[21]

As it is now more than sixty-two years since the Kensington Stone was found, there are not many men still alive who saw it right after it was found. It was therefore interesting to obtain the following statement from one of Olof Ohman's neighbors at that time. Mr. Moen is still in good health and employed in the office of the city clerk in Alexandria, Minnesota.

> Back in the 1890's I lived in Kensington and saw much of Olof Ohman. He often came to our house because my father did all the writing for him, both in English and Swedish. I also saw the runic stone that Ohman found and the stump of the tree that grew above the stone. This was only a few days after Ohman found the stone.
>
> Henry Moen
> April 18, 1955

Just after the manuscript of this book was sent to the publishers, a copy of a privately printed book of 77 pages was received from O. G. Lañdsverk, a scientist in Glendale, California. Dr. Lañdsverk felt that the circumstances of the discovery of the inscription were of paramount importance, and after thorough local study he has recorded them in much greater detail than any other writer. The book can be obtained from him without charge.

chapter seven

THE WEATHERING OF THE INSCRIPTION

The next attack by Wahlgren deals with the weathering of the inscription. He begins by criticizing the scholarship of Winchell and Upham because (he thinks) they were unable to weigh or measure the stone properly. He says:

> How did the geologists Upham and Winchell, the Museum Committee's petrographical experts, arrive at descriptions, on so easily obtainable matter as the weight and dimensions of the stone, that differed from each other and differed still more markedly from present-day descriptions of the stone? The difference between 29½ and 30 (or even 31) inches for the length is trifling; the difference between 36 and 30 is a cause for comment, as is the difference between 202 and 230 pounds.[1]

It is true that if the stone is measured down through the middle of the inscription, the length is 30 inches. But if a square box was made for it for shipment, that box would have to be 36 inches long, inside measurement, and that is probably how Winchell got his measurements.

The difference in weight cited by Wahlgren may well be due to faulty scales. Presumably Winchell and Upham did not themselves weigh the stone, but accepted other—and unfortunately undependable—reports of the weight. Moreover, it should be remembered that this stone, weighing more than two hundred pounds, is a very awkward object to carry around. One end is much heavier than the other, and when it was exhibited, it usually required the labor of three men.

The inscription is made on a stone which is called *graywacke*, and this is very hard rock. But the stone is partly covered with a layer of calcite, and this has largely weathered away so that the nine characters on this calcite show almost no depth. As a result, some of the letters are practically unreadable except for the context. In some cases the photographs have unfortunately been made clearer by retracing the letters in the calcite with a lead-pencil, but this gives a false impression of the state of the weathering.

Professor Winchell in his report presents a very clear report on the geological history of the Kensington Stone under the title, "The Slight Weathering of the Rune Stone."[2] He explains that it was once a part of a larger stone which split in two. He says:

> The calcite deposit that covers a part of it [the inscribed stone] was formed in a joint-opening before the stone was separated from its neighbor, and it has had approximately as long direct exposure to the elements as the rest of the surface. . . . It the slab was separated from its neighbor 548 years ago, it must have lain with its face side down during the most of that period. . . . If it was so separated fifteen or thirty years ago, it may have lain with its face side up and probably would show no more weathering than it now evinces. In short, there is no possible natural way to preserve that calcite scale from general disintegration for 548 years except to bury it beneath the surface. If it were not thus buried and still is intact, it must have been exposed and the inscription must have been made less than a hundred years ago, and probably less than thirty years ago. [See Figure 5 for runes in calcite.]

Professor Winchell has no doubt about how it lay. Four times in his report he states that the stone lay with its face down;[3] so also does Warren Upham.[4] Professor George T. Flom also admits this. In 1909 he made a personal visit to the finding place and talked with many persons there. When he returned to Illinois, he wrote his address to the Illinois State Historical Society, in which he says twice that the stone when unearthed lay with its face down.[5]

The position of the stone when found is not doubtful because all the reports and sworn statements by men who saw the stone before it was removed from the tree are in complete agreement. According to these eyewitnesss, neither side of the stone was visible before the tree was pulled down because the main roots converged on top of the stone to form the trunk of the tree. Then when the tree and the stump were overtuned, the face of the stone was revealed in a vertical position. The fact that the inscription was seen as soon as the tree and its roots were overturned shows that the stone was lying with its face down because the other side of the stone remained hidden by the main roots of the tree. In this position the inscription was not subject to any weathering because this takes place only at the surface of the ground. I have a letter from The Geological Survey of the Department of Interior reads thus:

> *The weathering of stones is mainly chemical and takes place only at the surface of the ground. The stones may, therefore, be perfectly fresh or unaltered until they are exposed for a time at the surface to the corrosive action of rainfall containing acids absorbed from the atmosphere and surface soils.* (Italics added) [6]

It has already been shown that the stone was lying in its finding place at least as long as the tree had been standing over it. This brings us back to 1856 or 1828, depending on whether the tree was a healthy, fast-growing tree or a sickly, stunted tree, as Ohman says. But in 1856 the earliest pioneers in Minnesota had only reached within ninety miles of the Kensington vicinity. Moreover, the seed of a tree could not have sprouted and begun to grow unless the stone was fully covered with soil. Under forest conditions, this accumulation of soil near the top of a hill would take a very long time. If on an open hillside it would be still longer.

As the stone weighs more than two hundred pounds, it is not likely that it has been moved between the time it was carved and its discovery. Moreover, it was during the early part of this period that the stone must have acquired the weathering which the geologists have commented upon. We cannot tell how it changed from its perpendicular to its horizontal position. As Professor Winchell says:[7]

> We cannot of course state how many forests have grown and been thrown down by tornados within the 548 years through which it may have been on the spot, nor how many buffaloes have rubbed against it; nor, finally, to what acts of violence the native Indians may have resorted to counteract its influence.

But it was not only Winchell who was persuaded of the great age of the inscription. All the geologists who have examined the inscription are convinced that the inscription was made long before the pioneers came. Dr. Warren Upham, who as secretary of the Minnesota Historical Society had the stone lying on a table in his office for a year and half, wrote:

> When we compare the excellent preservation of the glacial scratches shown on the back of the stone, which were made several thousand years ago, with the mellow, time-worn appearance of the face of the inscription, the conclusion is inevitable that the inscription must have been carved many hundred years ago.[8]

Upham's reference to the glacial scratches is significant. If this stone is so hard that the glacial striations are still visible after 7,000 years of exposure, it is not strange if the inscription shows relatively little wear after 600 years, most of which time it was covered up.

Wahlgren, speaking of himself, says: "The author, who first saw the Kensington Stone in 1953, was amazed at how new and fresh it looked fifty-five years after its discovery." He had no reason to be amazed because he mentions in the preceding paragraph how it happened. He says that Dr. R. H. Landon, Plant Physiologist of the University of Minnesota, had made three replicas of the Kensington Stone just before World War II, in the course of which work the stone was thoroughly coated with engine oil. In cleaning the stone afterwards, Dr. Landon says:

. . . several gallon of petroleum ether was used with the result that the Stone was cleaner than it ever had been. The oil softened any adherent material, and the ether carried it away. A careful inspection of the inscription, including use of microscope, showed a complete absence of any trace of weathering or patina. . . . The cuts were as fresh as if they had been made the day before.[9]

In 1910, Dr. W. O. Hotchkiss, later president of the Michigan School of Mines, wrote:

I have carefully examined the various phases of weathering on the Kensington Stone, and with all respect for the opinions of philologists, I am persuaded that the inscription cannot have been made in recent years. It must have been made at least fifty to a hundred years ago and perhaps earlier.[10]

Even some of the opponents of the inscription have admitted that the physical appearance of the inscription indicates great age. There was George O. Curme, chairman of the Germanic Department of Northwestern University, who had the stone in his office for two weeks in February, 1899, only three months after it was found. He subjected the inscription to repeated microscopic examinations and was inclined to believe that the inscription was authentic. He therefore wrote a couple of articles favoring that view. In the ensuing correspondence with Professor Breda, to whom he attributed superior knowledge of Norse linguistics, he deferred to Breda's insistence that the inscription was a fraud. But the physical evidence in the inscription continued to bother him. This is revealed in an interview dated March 3, 1899. In this he says:

The letters of the inscription were evidently carved with a sharp instrument for they are clear and distinct in outline. But the fact that the upper edge of the incised line is rough and rounded as a result of the disintegration of the stone, while the bottom of the incisions is sharp and clear, shows plainly that many years must have elapsed since the inscription was cut. In other words, the external appearance of the Kensington rune stone, so far from speaking against it, is such that the inscription may well be 600 years old.[11]

Commenting on this, Professor G. F. Hanson, state geologist of Wisconsin, says:[12]

> The statement of Prof. G. O. Curme that the upper edge of the incised line was rough and rounded indicates weathering to me. If you look at old rock exposures, you will note that blocks which were once obviously angular have had the corners rounded off tending to make them spheroidal. This type of weathering produces a physical effect.

It is an important fact that while the inscription has been examined by a dozen or more geologists, none of them has found any reason to doubt that it was made many years before the stone was found. Not so with the "H" which I, in 1908, chiseled at the lower end of the inscribed side. They all recognize this as a recent carving. To be sure, Dr. Bröndsted claims that this "H" shows a *beginning* of weathering (*en begyndende forvitringshud*). But if it takes fifty years for a greywacke to show a slight weathering, it would take more than a hundred years to show the complete weathering that Dr. Upham describes (see above).

chapter eight

THE REFERENCE TO "THIS ISLAND"

The inscription speaks of the finding place of the stone as an island "14 days' voyage from this island." No one would think of calling this elevation an island now, because it is merely a slight rise in a rolling, variegated landscape. Dr. Bröndsted, the eminent Danish archaeologist who visited this "island" in 1948, was much impressed by it. In 1951 he published a long report on the Kensington Stone and other finds, and in this report he mentions "the island" as follows:[1]

> The finding place is a bank situated in a long dried-up depression. There is a possibility that five hundred years ago this depression was a lake, over which the bank rose as an island. If this can be substantiated geologically, and if simultaneously it can be shown that there was no lake in the nineteenth century, this would be evidence in favor of the stone's genuineness. The question cannot be said to have been clarified so far, however.

Dr. Karl Martin Nielsen, who was requested by Dr. Bröndsted to discuss the philological aspects of the inscription, was also impressed by this mention of an island. He says:[2]

> The inscription contains two items which call for an explanation before it can be said that its origin as modern is proven by evidence. This is the mention of the finding place as "this island" and the year 1362. Can the first have been the result of intuitive fantasy?

The answers to these questions are as follows: There is abundant evidence to show that this elevation at one time was an island. It is shown by the fact that the floor of the large swamp surrounding it is perfectly flat, which is caused by the leveling action of the waves. It is also shown by the position of certain piles of rocks. Early in spring the ice close to the shore is the first to melt because the layer is thin. This creates an open space between the main sheet of the ice and the shore and permits a motion of the main sheet in what is called an ice-shove. This deposit of large boulders, pushed upward by the movement of a large sheet of ice, is about fifteen feet above the ancient floor of the lake, which shows that this former lake at one time was about fifteen feet deep.

But when the government surveyors came in 1866 (one year before the pioneers came in 1867), they found no lake. This is proven by the map in the field book of the surveyor made in 1866. This map (part of which is reproduced, see Figure 6) shows every important elevation, lake, swamp and watercourse, and the topography is precisely the same as it is now. Each square is a quarter section containing 160 acres. In the middle of the upper part of the map is seen "Sec. 14." Ohman's farm lies in the next lower quarter section to the right. The swamp to the northeast of the finding place is marked *dry*, and the steep part of the knoll where the stone was found is marked with a sign like a crescent. To change any part of this area into an island would require some tilting of the surface of the land. Is there any probability that any such disturbance of the topography has taken place?

Yes. It is a well-known fact that the greater northern part of the continent has been subject to many upheavals in the aftermath of the glacial invasion. When the last glacier spread a blanket of ice, many thousand feet thick, over Canada and many of the northern states of North America, this tremendous weight depressed the surface of the earth hundreds of feet, according to the thickness of the glacial ice. Later, when the ice melted, the surface of the earth rose up again in a series of spasmodic upheavals because of the decrease in the enormous pressure above it. In most places little is known of the height of these upheavals, but in northwestern Minnesota we have very specific information because of the fact that the broad Red River valley was once a great glacial lake. This is all made very clear in Dr. Warren Upham's admirable work, *Glacial Lake Agassiz*. The valley extended from the continental divide at Brown's Valley, Minnesota, and slopes northward about four hundred miles to Lake Winnipeg. When the southern part of the glacier melted, the valley became a vast lake because the outlet to the north remained closed for a very long period. This former lake left thirty-one broad and high beaches which mark the boundaries of the lake at successive periods.

These beach-lines are not precisely horizontal as would be expected, but have an upward tilt to the north averaging a little more than a foot per mile. Thus we find the great Herman beach, which marks the highest altitude of the glacial lake, is 1,055 feet above the sea at Lake Traverse, the southern outlet of Lake Agassiz, and 1,182 feet at Maple Lake, 120 miles farther north in a straight line. These measurements prove that the earth's crust at a much later time was subjected to a series of uplifts which raised it 127 feet in this distance.

According to Dr. Upham, each of these 31 successive beaches is the result of a new upheaval because they are not truly parallel with each other, but follow slightly different angles of incline. There are also some irregularities in the altitude of the beaches which indicate minor local disturbances.

These many upheavals and other disturbances took many thousand years as they successively built up very wide and high beaches (300 to 400 feet wide and 15 to 20 feet high) and also vast deltas covering hundreds of square miles. The latest uplift may therefore well have taken place within the last 500 years. In fact, Professors L. E. Martin, F. T. Thwaites and Dr. Warren Upham all say that these upheavals and tiltings are going on at the present time. Professor Martin writes:

> The tilting of the land which had covered the inclination of the beaches and the submergence of the western part of the shoreline of the Nipissing Great Lakes may be still in progress. This was first noticed more than 75 years ago and was afterward studied more carefully, so that we now know something about the rate at which the tilting is going on. To say that a line 100 miles long and trending approximate-

ly north-south, is being tilted at such a rate that the southern end of it will be four or five inches below the northern end after the lapse of a century seems to indicate a very slow movement. It may turn out, however, that the tilting is spasmodic, with intervals of movement interrupted by intervals of rest. However this may be, the slow tilting has sufficed to submerge the stumps of trees near Superior, where the trees, of course, grew above lake level. The tilting has submerged rapids during the lifetime of some of the Indians, as indicated in the beginning of this chapter.[3]

As the Kensington Stone was found in an area closely contiguous to a region which shows much evidence of repeated tiltings, both spasmodic and gradual, this appears fully to explain the disappearance of this lake near the Ohman home. Professor Winchell says:

I am convinced from the geological conditions and the physical changes which the region has experienced, probably during the last 500 years, that the stone contains a genuine record of a Scandinavian exploration into Minnesota, and must be accepted as such for the date named.[4]

chapter nine

LINGUISTIC OBJECTIONS

When the first translations of the Kensington inscription were made by Breda and Rygh, it was believed to contain English words. This theory was rejected by Professor Flom, the first philologist in America to study the inscription. It is also rejected by Wahlgren and other opponents in America, but many of the philologists in the Scandinavian countries still base their opposition on the assumption that the words *mans, from, ded* and *illy* reflect the vernacular of a Norse emigrant after a few years' residence in America.[1]

It is true that there is a considerable mixture of common English words in the speech of a Norwegian-American farmer. His vocabulary is rather limited, and it is natural that such common words as *barn, stable, field, crop, dinner, acre* were quickly adopted in the Norwegian speech; but serious and solemn words were rarely adopted. As prepositions have no meaning by themselves, they were never adopted, and *from* never became a part of the hybrid language of the immigrants. Nor did *mans* because there is no such word in English except in the possessive case. Fritzner gives the following definition of *man*: "The occupants of a household including children, slaves and other employes; also in collective meaning."[2] The same word, spelled *mans*, occurs frequently in the old sagas in the meaning of *men, people*, and is still so used in Iceland. It is also found in a Swedish letter of 1349: "Han ok hans äruinge skal that goz aghä . . . som twer gother mäns . . . sighia."[3] In the Kensington inscription it occurs twice, first in the sentence "[wi] fan 10 *man*," and then, later, "[we] har 10 *mans*."

Professor S. N. Hagen thinks that "the use of both forms in one inscription indicates that *mans* had not yet been altogether displaced by *man* and that both were current in the inscriber's dialect," which seems a plausible explanation. He adds that the variation *10 man: 10 mans* within the same inscription is no more improbable than the variation *30 men* (acc): *30 manna* (gen.) within the same short chapter of *Egils Saga* in almost identical sentences."[4]

The word *ded* is almost always the first word pointed to by Scandinavian critic-scholars as proof that the Kensington inscription is the work of some Swedish or Norwegian hoaxer who spoke a mixture of English and a Scandinavian tongue. But, as stated above, serious words relating to death and judgment were seldom a part of the language mixture. Professor Kock of Lund University in Sweden has a better explanation. He points out that the preserved documents from the late Middle Ages are very weak in phonetics and gives a large number of illustrations of the use of *e* for *ö* and vice versa.[5] Even among the best educated of that time, we find numerous examples of this confusion. We still have the original of a letter written from Lödöse by Queen Margareta, in which she or her secretary spells this name *Ledese!* Later in this letter she also misspels the very word under discussion—*ded!* She writes: "Effther the henne husbonde her Jens Herne *ded* er" (as her husband, Sir Jens Herne, is dead).[6] Thus we have three instances where *e* is substituted for *ö* in one short letter.

Finally we come to *illy* or *illu*. There is some about whether the last letter is a *u* or *y*. In either case the word is here used as a dative singular neuter, meaning *evil*. As *illu* is the correct dative form as illustrated in the Lord's Prayer of about 1300: *frälse os af illu* (save us from evil), it would seem that this is what the runemaster intended to write. On the other hand, it appears that the dative form changed from *illu* to *illi* very early. This is illustrated in the refrain of an ancient poem from the time of the Black Plague of 1349-50 which reads:

Hjälpe os Gud a Maria Möy,
A frälsä oss alle av *illi*.
(Help us God and Virgin Mary
And save us all from evil).

The use of *y* for *i* is very common both in accented and unaccented syllables.

Professor Flom's theory was that the inscription was the work of a man who was familiar with the Dalecarlian runes.[7] This theory is rejected by Wahlgren, and the impossibility of it hase been fully demonstrated.[8]

In the inscription the sign þ occurs fourteen times, and in my interpretation I read this sign as *d*. Professor Flom objected strenuously to this and claimed that this sign in the fourteenth century was a dental spirant which always stood for *th* or *dh*.[9] However, Professor Hagen[10] has shown that in the old West Gothland Law which dates from about 1285, there is a long list of words in which þ is used for *d*. This objection is now forgotten, and even Wahlgren rejects it.[11]

Wahlgren also rejects, "for semantic reasons," the claim made by two Danish philologists that the form *rise* for *rese* shows that the runemaster was an immigrant who "mixed" his language. Professor D. A. Seip gives a better explanation. He says that "palatal consonants often tend to a preservation of *i* (thus often in the form *Noregi*).[12] Professor Schlyter says that Lydikinus often wrote *i* for *e* (see Västgötalagen, p. ix.) In Queen Margareta's letter to the king of 1370 we find *ider* for *eder*, *bider* for *beder*, *smyd* for *smed*, etc.

Surprisingly, the inscription begins without any sentence subject. This is also the case in the sentence on the flat edge of the stone and in the sentence (*vi*) *fan*. Professors Falk and Torp state that the omission of personal pronouns in the subject of the sentence is characteristic of writings of the fourteenth century, and Professor Nygaard has written an exhaustive dissertation on this subject.[13]

The first word in the inscription is *Göter*, which refers to the inhabitants of East and West Gothland in the southern part of Sweden: Swedish plurals have so long been characterized by the ending *ar* that the spelling *göter* seems strange. But in the *old* writings we find that the ending *er* is often used in the thirteenth and fourteenth centuries. Lydikinus, a priest of West Gothland, about the year 1300 wrote some annotations to the *Västgötalag*. Commenting on his style, Schlyter says: "Instead of

the endings *a* and *ar* we find almost everywhere *ä* and *är*."[14]
Other references are given in Holand, *Westward from Vinland*,
1940, p. 290.

The second letter in *göter* is carved on the stone with two
dots above it. This has been criticized because the public
scriveners who wrote the letters for the common people used
only one dot. But among the Germans, the umlauts of *o*, and
also the *a* and *u*, were written with two dots above.[15] Professor
P. A. Munch says that in the fourteenth century practically all
the merchants in Oslo, Bergen and Stockholm were Germans.
A letter from Queen Margareta (1370) shows that her household, including the Royal Bodyguard, obtained their household
necessities from a German merchant named Westfal in Oslo.[16]
No doubt invoices were sent with the goods, and if these showed
double dots over the *a*, *o* and *u*, they would gradually be adopted
and soon became widely used.

There have been so many ill-advised philological arguments
against the inscription that Wahlgren finds it necessary to dis-
sociate himself from them. He says,

> The present investigation [his own] does not endorse or
> take responsibility for all the linguistic arguments that have
> been proferred in this direction, for these have varied con-
> siderably in accuracy, merit and importance.[17]

Wahlgren calls attention to the fact that while most of the
letters that have been preserved from the Middle Ages are
characterized by frequent grammatical and sonorous inflections,
we find little of this in the Kensington inscription. This is quite
true, but there is a reason for this difference. In those days there
were no common schools, and few persons could read or write.
As one of the principal sources of income for the church was
through testamentary gifts, it was of prime importance that
these gifts were properly recorded and witnessed. Of similar
importance were the conveyances of real estate. In order that
these documents should be properly drawn up, the Bishop was
instructed to appoint a monk in each parish to act as notary
public. These notaries were aged monks, diplomatic and ex-

perienced, and as they dealt chiefly with legal papers which were carefully preserved, the latter make up the bulk of the letters from the Middle Ages. To impress the common man with the dignity of his product, these letters had a solemn and authoritative structure, still favored by many members of the legal profession, abounding in old-fashioned phrases and formulas.[18]

But this was not the speech of the common people in the middle of the fourteenth century. As Professor Munch says:

> The languages of the two kingdoms [Sweden and Norway], which had always much resembled each other, were now [because of the Union in 1319] in the process of amalgamation. The numerous [Swedish] clergy appointed to Norway, the many new connecting links, and the constant association between Norwegians and Swedish families, caused the spoken language, and in part the written language, of the upper classes of Norway to approach that of the Swedes. . . . The melodious and highly inflected Old Norse language was being displaced by a less elegant transition language, marked by lacerated word forms and the lack of strict grammatical rules and therefore probably not written the same way by any two writers. In part it resembled Old Norse, in part Swedish, and in part the provincial dialects. . . . *The regular grammatical inflections* which distinguish all old languages *were the first to be discarded.* (Italics added.) . . . The neglect of inflectional endings and the substitution of particles or the use of certain modified sentence structures became characteristic.[19]

Falk and Torp also dwell on the disintegration of the sonorous Old Norse language, as shown in the writings of the fourteenth century. They add that "there are numerous examples showing that many dialects in the fourteenth century had given up plural verb forms."[20]

There is one big difficulty in identifying the dialectic origin of the Kensington inscription. This is the fact that these thirty men "from Vinland" were not from one district, but represented many far separated parts of Norway and Sweden, and possibly even of Skåne, each of which had its own dialect. For many years these men had been living together in intimate association.

It is therefore almost certain that their respective dialects would be somewhat modified by their long contact.

It is not likely that the writing of the sons and daughters of the upper classes would be influenced by the antique style of the old monks who acted as public notaries. They would have private teachers. Below I present three letters written about 1370. The spelling, to be sure, shows many vagaries, but when they are read aloud, we find in them the same diction as in the Kensington inscription.

The first is written by Henrik Henrikson, a Swedish priest who was the king's seal-bearer and later chancellor. The original is preserved and is dated 1371. It is printed in *Diplomatarium Norwegicum*, Vol. VI, No. 278.

> Min aldrakæreste herra konung Hakon. Jech helsar yder med gudh oc med minne ødhmyuke þienest, kungør jach jder at erkebiscopin aff Þrondeim dødhe jnnan gaar vm nat hær j Oslo, oc herra Sighurder comber ey aff siengenne fore øginawerk, . . .

The following part of a long letter is reproduced by photograph of the original which is still preserved. It was written at Akershus, Oslo, in 1392 by Queen Margareta to her husband, King Haakon Magnussen: It is printed in *Diplomatarium Norwegicum*, Vol. 1, No. 409.

> Jdhir min aldrakærasta herra, helsar jak Margareta jnnerligha med gudh, kungør iak ider at jak ma væll gud late mik thet sama till ider spøria, vita skulin j thet min kære herra, at jak ok mine thiænara liidhum stora nøødh, vm mat oc dryk, swa at hwargæ iak ælla the fangom vara nøødthorfft. Oc thy bider iak ider min kære herra, at j finnin ther nokra vægha till at thet møge bættras, at the som med mik æra, ey skulu skylias vider mek fore hungers skuld ok bider iak ider at j scriuin till Væstfall at han mik møghe borgha thet sem iak kan honomtilsigia oc viderthorua, oc sighin honom at j vilin honom væll bytala thet sem han mik borghar.

The third letter was written by Tubbe Erikssön, one of King Magnus' faithful officers in West Gothland in 1372. The original is preserved and printed in *Diplomatarium Norwegicum*, Vol. IV. No. 501.

Konog Magnus ok konog Hacon med gutz naat konogga j Norreghe ok Suereke helsar jak Tubbe Erekson *ødmiu med guth kunger jak jther thes at jak ær scild af Ørabro, ok ligger jak ok bithar een suar af thetta bref vm j vilen mina thyænest haua ok vilen j mik nokot vnna j Vestragøtland tel Noreghes vil jak ey ok jak kan ey legge vacta for thy jak hauer myket folk huat j vilen mik gøra. thet kungøren mik med thenna brefførrara vel hauer jak andra vtuægha vtan jak vil eygh annat bigripa før een jak hauer hort jthar villia. scriptum anno domini . . .

In the fourteenth century there were no rules for spelling in Norway or Sweden. The orthography of these letters is therefore strange. But when read aloud, they will at once be recognized as being written in the dialect of the region around Oslofjord and southeastward to and around the present Gothenborg.

Wahlgren points to the use in the inscription of singular verbs for the plural and says this was great rarity, particularly in Swedish formal documents. Well, that is the last place where we would expect them because, as I have already pointed out, the notary publics who drew up the documents persistently clung to the old forms. Professor D. A. Seip in his *Norsk Sproghistorie inntil 1370* writes: "Singular verbs were used for plural even before 1300, and oftener and oftener in the first half of the fourteenth century."[21] As people cling longer to old-fashioned forms when writing than when speaking, it is easy to understand that the colloquial speech of the members of this expedition of 1362 would be ultra-modern for their time.

By the middle of the fourteenth century, the neglect of plural verb forms had become so common in Norwegian manuscripts that Falk and Torp say: "There are numerous examples showing that many dialects had given up plural verb forms."[22] Professor Gustav Indrebö has written a dissertation entitled "Some Remarks on the Disappearance of the Plural in the Conjugation of Verbs in Norwegian," supported by scores of fourteenth-century quotations.[23] Likewise Professor Bröndum-

Nielsen has shown that *Den Skånske Lov* of about 1250 frequently uses singular verbs with plural subjects.[24] For other examples see my book, *The Kensington Stone*, 1932, pp. 235-36.

One word which Wahlgren finds highly suspicious is *opdagelse*. He says that the word *uppdaga* "to find," is recorded in that sense in Sweden beginning in the nineteenth century. A passive form *uppdages* is recorded for the eighteenth century in the meaning "to grow light, dawn."[25]

If he means that it does not appear until the eighteenth century, he is mistaken. More than six hundred years earlier the root of the word, *daga*, was in common use in the meaning "to grow light, to be revealed, and dawn." In *Alvismal*, one of the Elder Edda poems, we read: "Uppi er tu nu dvergr *um dagadr* (Italics added), nu skinn sol i sali." Transposing the words of the first clause, we have: "Nu ert tu uppidagadr, nu skinn sol i sali." *Now you are revealed, the sun is shining,* which means "you are revealed." This refers to the old myth that the goblins of darkness turned to stone when caught by the light of day.[26]

Some of the ancient dialects in Norway, like in Telemarken, have used this word transitively for centuries in the meaning *to reveal.* "De kan da oppendage dikkon," said a farmer in Telemarken after some young men had crowded into his house on Christmas Eve, their faces covered with masks—"You might as well reveal yourselves." It may be that this is the sense of the word in the inscription. These travelers may have thought of their journey as being more a passive revealing than an active exploring. We have a word of cognate meaning in the English *discover*, which is derived from the old French *decouvrir*, to be uncovered," "to come to light." Professor Knut Söderwall, who as compiler of a three-volume dictionary of medieval Swedish words, had no doubt that *opdage* as a transitive verb was in use in the fourteenth century. I spent a couple of pleasant hours with him in his home in Lund, and he gave me the following statement:

> As far as I know, this word is not found in the meager literary fragments of the fourteenth century. But that proves nothing. As you probably know, these fragments consist chiefly of legal documents and homilies, and it is therefore

not strange if a word of such comparatively rare import as *opdagelse* is not found in such writings. The Old Norse word for this idea was *leita landa,* but this expression had become obsolete when the great change from Old Swedish to the Swedish of the late Middle Ages took place about 1300. As *landaleita* was dropped, some other term must have been adopted to express the same thought. The only word we know which fills this function is *opdage.*

Professor Söderwall was a most frank and friendly man with whom it was a great pleasure to speak. But I had taken up two hours of his time and I rose to leave. I had brought a photograph of the stone and a transliteration of the inscription which were lying on his deak. Pointing to the latter, I said: "Just one more question, Professor. What do you find in that inscription which is not compatible with fourteenth-century usage?"

He picked up the paper and studied it carefully, many minutes. Then he said: "There is one point which may be troublesome. It is the preposition *po* which comes from *upa.* The *u* was early elided because of its lack of accent and *pa* remained. Now I doubt if this *pa* changed to *på* or *po* as early as the middle of the fourteenth century. However, phonetics is not my forte and I may be wrong. If you will go upstairs in this building, you will find Professor Axel Kock, the greatest authority on Swedish phonetics. He will know."

I thanked him, and in a couple of minutes I was in Professor Kock's office and told him of Söderwall's question. He picked up the first volume of his *Fornsvensk Ljudlära* published in 1886. "I say here," he said, "that 'the change of the long *a* to long *å* was accomplished in the first half of the fifteenth century'—but I think I have something else on that." Then he picked up the first volume of his *Svensk Ljudhistoria,* published in 1906, and read "Dialectically the change of long *a* to *å* took place by the middle of the XIV century, at least, when accompanied by a labial consonant."

This comment has particular significance because *p* is a labial consonant. Incidentally, it shows how hopeless it would be for anyone to attempt to forge a long runic inscription. The linguistic difficulties are too many. One very prominent opponent, Dr. Erik Moltke of the National Museum in Copenhagen, realizes this and says:

> There are many opinions on both sides. Some experts say that the inscription is genuine while others say it is false, and it would be difficult to appraise one expert's qualifications above another. One thing is certain, however, and that is that it has not been proven that the inscription is false, nor has it been proven that it is genuine. Speech is a peculiar living fish, and it is not given to many desk philologists to get a true grasp on it. What do we know about the spoken language of the fourteenth century? Very, very little, and that little which we think we know we quarrel about. We must turn to the runes, and there, I believe, lies the solution.[27]

The clearest summation of the linguistic aspects of the inscription is by Professor S. N. Hagen. He writes:

> This inscription should be a perfect joy to the linguist because it is such a delightfully honest and unsophisticated record of its author's own speech. A forger would have tried to imitate a language other than his own. It is clear that this author tried to imitate no language but his own. In branding this beautiful inscription as a forgery, scholars have thrown away not only an important historical document, but also a faithful record of medieval Scaadinavian speech. It is fortunately of considerable length, and this has made it possible to test its authenticity at a very considerable number of points[28]

Evidently Wahlgren takes much the same view of the futility of the linguistic objections as does Dr. Moltke because he says: "the present investigation does not endorse or take responsibility for all the linguistic arguments that have been proffered in this direction, for these have varied considerably in accuracy, merit and importance."[29]

chapter ten

RUNIC OBJECTIONS

When Olof Ohman was a young boy there were no school facilities for children of the lower classes in his part of Sweden. There was a perambulatory school, held in successive farmhouses for six weeks each year. The children sat on the floor; there were neither desks, blackboards nor slates, and subjects requiring such facilities, such as writing and arithmetic, were not taught. Reading and religion were the two important lines of learning, and these were taught with the aid of a bible history, describing the great men of the Old Testament and the life and miracles of Jesus in the New Testament. Ohman had nine years of these six-weeks sessions, or nine months in all.

For the purpose of supplementing this meager schooling, a scholarly educator named Carl Rosander compiled a book entitled *Den Kunskapsrike Skolmästaren* (The Well-Informed Schoolmaster). This book contains chapters on arithmetic, bookkeeping, grammar, history, farming, and other subjects, and was a very useful book for persons with limited schooling. Ohman acquired this book in 1891, whether new or secondhand is not known. I did not see this book when I was in his house in 1909, but later I had an opportunity to study it at leisure.

This book is the subject of a chapter in Wahlgren's book entitled "A Certain Printed Book." Wahlgren begins his remarks with the statement: "One is struck instantly by the much-finger-marked pages 61-64 of the Rosander volume." Whether this is now true, I do not know; many people may have fingered these pages in recent years. Certainly, however, when I first inspected the book there were none. The only finger marks in the book were on the pages devoted to the history of Sweden in the latter part of the book.

From this chapter in Rosander's book, Wahlgren cites a number of linguistic and phonetic changes in the Swedish language in the fourteenth century, due in part to the commercial influence of the Hanseatic League. If the Kensington inscription did not agree essentially with Rosander in these developments, Wahlgren would undoubtedly and properly have claimed that the inscription was a fraud. But he admits that the inscription is in close agreement with Rosander, and then claims that "the forger" had borrowed his learning from Rosander! As a clinching argument he points out that the prayer on the stone—"Save (us) from evil"—is the same as Rosander quotes from the fourteenth century and therefore claims that the inscription is a fake!

This is not true. Below is given the complete runic alphabet of sixteen characters as printed in Rosander's book,[1] and below that is printed the runic alphabet of the Kensington Stone. A comparison of the two will show that the Kensington Stone has no less than sixteen signs which are not found in Rosander's alphabet.

In the tenth and eleventh centuries a new art was developed in the Scandinavian countries. This was the art of engraving highly artistic obituaries on big rocks. Hundreds of skilled stone cutters not only produced a new and fine art, but they also introduced a new and short alphabet of sixteen letters in contrast to the earlier alphabet of twenty-four letters.

There are still in existence hundreds of these short-alphabet inscriptions, but when Christianity was introduced, the Church frowned upon this practice because it was of heathen origin, and the Latin alphabet succeeded the runic. While there still were many friends of the old runemasters, there were many letters in the Latin alphabet which lacked runic equivalents, and this made necessary the invention of new signs.

This we see illustrated in Figure 8 which shows how the old standard runic alphabet had degenerated. The Scanian Law (third column) which was written about 1325 has an alphabet which is very much like that of the Kensington Stone which is dated 1362. The other two alphabets in Figure 8 which are of much later date show a great disparity with the old runic masters. The fact that the Kensington inscription does not in all points agree with the runic alphabet of 1000 A.D. is therefore only an example of the general decay of former standards in this field.

Up to about 1300 A.D. the Roman numerals were in use in western and northern Europe, being a legacy left by the Church. Then (or earlier) a new system was invented in the Scandinavian countries. It was closely related to the Arabic, but it had no sign for zero. It was well adapted for runic writing, each number having a perpendicular staff, and the value of each number was indicated by a horizontal line.

We are indebted to a prominent Danish scholar by the name of Ole Worm, for information about the use of runic numerals. In 1643 he published a work in Latin, entitled *Fasti Danici*, in which he shows the use of these numerals in 1328. This work has not been translated and is very rare. Professor Worm discusses the ancient *primstaver* (also called *runstaver*) or household almanacs, which were in use in the Scandinavian countries in the late Middle Ages. This perpetual calendar usually consisted of a flat stick of wood, like a yardstick, on which were marked the necessary symbols and also signs for holy days which, all together, enabled the owner to determine the date. Figure 9 shows a page from Worm's book which gives the symbols used to designate the numbers 1 to 19. Here, in column 3, we see the same system as is used in the inscription, the only difference being that the numbers from 10 to 20 are marked with a cross-bar at the top, while the inscription shows a circle—both of these signs representing 10. Figure 10 shows a comparison of Worm's numerals with those on the Kensington Stone.

These runic numerals from the primstaver were just as adaptable for decimal notation as are the Arabic numerals. We have an excellent record of the early use of the decimal system in a manuscript entitled *Algorismus*—a treatise on numbers—a Norse manuscript of about 1320. Professor P. A. Munch[3] has given a complete translation of this treatise. As decimal notation was known in the North in the early part of the fourteenth century, it is likely that some of the more intelligent and better educated men, like the members of the King's

Bodyguard, were also familiar with decimal notation in 1362. The Kensington Stone gives three numbers in decimal notation, 14, 22 and 1362.

Dr. Erik Moltke of the National Museum, Copenhagen, is the principal critic of the runes in the Kensington inscription. While he rejects all linguistic objections, he says the inscription cannot be older than 1550 because it contains a *j* and an *ö*, both of which—so he asserts—were not invented until then.

This objection is hardly valid because there is no way of telling when a letter or sign was invented—no one bothered to record the invention.

We know that the consonantal sound of the letter *j* was familiar to the Norse people because they had a runic sign for it in the older and fuller runic alphabet of twenty-four characters in use from about 200 to 900 A.D. Then when the later runic alphabet of sixteen signs was adopted, *e, i* and *j* were all represented by an i.

In the greater part of Europe there was no *j* because the Latin alphabet which was introduced with Christianity had none. But Adolf Noreen, Sweden's greatest philologist says: "In the Swedish manuscripts from the 14th century and even earlier, the sign *j* is not uncommon."[4] Professors Otto von Friesen and Axel Kock both say that *j* as a consonant was in use in Middle Swedish (1300-1533).[5]

From the fourteenth to the eighteenth centuries the *i* and *j* were used, mostly indiscriminately, both as sonants and consonants. In my translation of the Kensington inscription where it occurs once, I translated it as a consonant, because I was translating into modern usage. It now remains to look into the origin of the sign which in the inscription is used for a *j*.

The answer is that this form of the letter was in use in the fourteenth century. In *King Waldemar's Jordebog* from about 1300 A.D., the writer's name, Jon, is written with the sign ⱦ which is a reversed copy of the rune in the inscription.[6] Such reversed runes are common. But the runemaster may not have reversed the sign. In Norway, Sweden and Iceland, the *j* with the oblique line on the *right* was common. In the *Flatey Book*, largely compiled by a Norwegian, Magnus Thorhallsson, about 1380, this sign in cursive writing is often used.

The sign ⊦ is also found in cursive form in many letters from the fourteenth century. As an illustration may be cited Queen Margareta's letter of 1370 where it occurs twenty-two times. Its form in cursive writing is ℐ as shown in the first letter of the first word of the letter, as shown in the first letter of the first word of Queen Margareta's letter of 1370, printed in Figure 11 of this book. The upward curve to the left is merely ornamental and means no more than the curve to the left in the modern cursive capitals ℐ, ℛ, and ℬ. If this curve is omitted, we have ℐ basically the same sign as in the inscription, (⊦), the oblique line and the cross line being made by one swing of the pen.

The runic alphabet was in wide use in the Scandinavian countries until in the eleventh and twelfth centuries when it was supplanted by the Latin alphabet upon the introduction of Christianity. In the course of time the Latin alphabet was found lacking in signs for certain umlauts. This made it desirable to introduce new signs. In the Kensington inscription we find two such new signs— ⊛ and ⋇. The former sign has been the subject of considerable criticism.

For a long time there was no uniformity in the use of these signs. Manuscripts of the fourteenth century show no less than ten ways of writing the letter ö, and there are some writers who use two or three forms on the same page without any difference in sound.[7] The most common forms were *o* with with one dot above, *o* with an oblique bisecting line and a circumflex above, and *o* with a cross in the middle. The first was the simplest and should therefore have become the survivor but it did not. Why was this?

The explanation is probably a strong foreign influence. In Germany in the fourteenth century it was customary to mark umlauts with two dots above *a*, *o* and *u*.[8] In the 1300's the Hanseatic League had a powerful influence in commerce in the North, and German accountants presumably used the double dots in their invoices. In this way they would become known to

those members of the King's Bodyguard whose daily task it was
to keep the king's large household supplied with food, clothing
and equipment of all kinds. We know from the queen's letter
of 1370 that the royal household in Oslo bought all its supplies
from a German merchant named Westfal.[9] The rapid dominance
in the writing of this sign is fully explained by its introduction
through the Hansa merchants.

Dr. Moltke has other objections. Speaking of perpetual
calendars, to which reference has been made above, he says:

> If we inspect these calendars, we find, especially in those
> from the 16th and 17th centuries, that they operate with
> greatly degenerated runic alphabets which have forms not
> unlike those of the Kensington Stone. *There cannot there-
> fore be the slightest doubt* that the writer of the Kensington
> inscription has constructed his alphabet from the alphabet
> of such a Swedish runic calendar.[10]

I made a brief reply to this, and Dr. Moltke the next year
was good enough to admit that he was following a false trail.
He wrote:[11]

> Have we shown that the inscription is false? Not at all;
> for while the degenerated calendar runes appear to belong
> to the 15th and 16th centuries, we cannot ignore the fact
> that Ole Worm's calendar was from 1328. We have reached
> that borderland of doubt which is the particular element of
> this inscription. The alphabet does not seem probable for
> the 14th century, but on the other hand it is impossible
> to disprove it.
>
> Precisely the same point do we come to when we turn to
> the numerals. Even in the late medieval inscriptions, dates
> are expressed either by Roman numerals or the number is
> written out with runes . . . but Holand has succeeded in
> finding in the parchment literature examples of very early
> use of Arabic numbers.

Dr. Moltke also found fault with the form of the rune for *n*.
He claimed that the ᚼ which is used on the stone was superseded
by ᚾ. He overlooks the fact that in West Gothland, where the

runemaster probably came from, may still be seen scores of old runestones, and most of them use the form ⸕ for n. Dr. Moltke, who is a reasonable man, saw that his objection was not valid, and in his reply he says: "It is not wise to lay emphasis on this form."[12]

In the study of late runic forms, Moltke could well say that it is not wise to lay emphasis on *any* form. From about 1200 there were no accepted standard forms in writing runic inscriptions because runic writing had almost ceased. Figure 8 shows the alphabets of three well-known medieval inscriptions in parallel columns together with the alphabet of the Kensington Stone. The comparison shows the following differences: (1) There is a minimum of similarity between the Kensington and the Dalarne alphabets. (2) The Scanian Law of about 1300 shows almost the same differences from the Ihre-Götlin and Liljegren alphabets as does the Kensington alphabet. (3) The Scanian Law differs from the Kensington alphabet in only seven characters. If Flom was seeking an alphabet similar to that of the Kensington Stone, why did he pass by the Scanian Law where there are only seven divergences and select the Dalarne alphabet where there are twice as many?

On February 28, 1899, the *Svenska Amerikanska Posten* had a report on the finding of the Kensington Stone. In this report the *Posten* says: "Mr. Ohman made a copy of the inscription and sent this through J. P. Hedberg to the *Svenska Amerikanska Posten*. We therefore sent it to Professor O. J. Breda." Following this early report, I wrote in my *Explorations in America* that Ohman made a copy of the inscription which J. P. Hedberg sent to the Swedish paper.

This was an error because Hedberg in a letter to Professor Winchell dated March 12, 1910, says that he (Hedberg) made the copy that was sent to the *Posten*. But this copy (see Fig.12) was not printed in the *Posten*. Instead, it printed the Sieverts copy which had been sent to Breda. The Hedberg copy was sent to the Swedish paper on January 1, 1899. The editor apparently was not favorably impressed with Hedberg's carelessly written letter and slovenly copy of a strange inscription and took no steps to publish it for two months. Then, when reports of this find appeared in the Minneapolis *Tribune* and other papers, he apparently felt the necessity of doing something about it. He, therefore, called on Breda to get his opinion about the significance of this find. Thus he learned about the Siverts copy of the inscription. This was much better suited for publication than Hedberg's inexact copy, and he obtained the use of the Siverts copy from Breda. It is doubtful if Hedberg's own copy was published until forty years later. Then J. A. Holvik found it in the archives of the Minnesota Historical Society, and he printed a photostat of it in the Moorhead *Concordian*, November 18, 1949, claiming that it was the *draft* from which the Kensington inscription was copied. In the meantime more or less exact copies of the inscription were published in the Chicago *Tribune* February 21, 1899, and Chicago *Skandinaven*, February 24, 1899.

Wahlgren admits that "the Hedberg sketch contains nearly a score of recognizable differences from the inscription,"[13] and yet he claims that Hedberg's copy was a draft for the guidance of the expert who inscribed the stone! There are also other evidences of haste. It was written on paper over a lined penmanship guide, and the lines are irregular. They are about three-sixteenths of an inch apart, and each alternate line was left unwritten to give proper space for the inscribed lines. Hedberg succeeded well with the three first lines, but in his haste he forgot to keep the next line open with the result that lines three and four of the copy collided. In line eight he became confused and crossed out A V M, although he had these letters in the proper place. All in all, this "draft" would have been a most impossible and unsatisfactory pattern for any forger to follow.

The first line shows other evidence that Hedberg's version is a copy of the inscription and not an earlier draft. It shows that the last four letters *o, p, d, a* (transliterated) have been rubbed out and then rewritten in the beginning of the second line. Why was this done? There was plenty of room for them in the first line. The reason, no doubt, was that Hedberg meant to make an exact copy, as he says, line for line. Then, when he had finished the first line, he saw that the inscription had these four letters in the second line, and he dutifully tried to erase them. If the Hedberg script were a draft and not a copy, there would be no reason for rubbing out these four signs.

Holvik's and Wahlgren's principal reasons for claiming that Hedberg's transcript is a draft are the following:

(1) On the runepaper [Hedberg's copy] the word for *fro* is written *fro* the first time it appears and *from* in the fourth line, while the stone has *fro* in both places.

(2) On the runepaper the word for *röd* is written with an H rune after the vowel. There is no H rune in the same word on the stone.

(3) The word for *blood* is spelled with a complicated character for the *umlaut* of *o* (ö) which is an incorrect spelling in any Scandinavian language at any time.

This is quite true. No one would write *blöd,* an adjective meaning *soft,* for *blod,* meaning *blood,* which shows that Hedberg did not know the meaning of what he was writing. Certainly the writer of the inscription did not use it as a draft because none of the seventeen mistakes in Hedberg's copy was transferred to the inscription. The only logical conclusion is that the Hedberg's copy of the inscription was made by a man who did not understand what he was copying.

Rygh's translation in Oslo indicates that he had been sent a copy *like* Hedberg's. It could hardly have been Hedberg's own copy because this original was preserved in the archives of the Minnesota Historical Society. The Swedish paper obtained the Sieverts copy (and published it) in exchange for the Hedberg copy, and it is therefore possible that Breda or one of his students made a copy of Hedberg's copy and sent it to Professor Rygh. A copy, somewhat like the Hedberg copy, was also printed in the Chicago *Tribune* February 21, 1899, but not with the same line arrangement. This was duplicated in *Skandinaven,* February 24, 1899. One of these "Hedberg" copies may be the copy that Rygh transliterated. He did not wait to check the words in the inscription and thus increased the confusion about the inscription.

It is not easy to copy a long document containing strange characters without making mistakes. All the early newspaper copies were faulty. This is also shown by Wahlgren's reprint of the Kensington inscription on the end papers of his book on the Kensington Stone. Although he has been busy with this inscription for several years, he makes no less than four mistakes in the first half of the inscription. The fourth sign in the third line of Wahlgren's copy is not an *l* as used in the inscription but a *d* in reversed position as used in the Scanian Law. The sixth sign in the fourth line is a cross with three dots. There is no such sign in the inscription. The *a* has one dot or hook, the *ä* has two dots, but where does he get that third dot? In the fifth line in the word *norr* he adds three dots where none is wanted. Of course, this is only a question of dots, but they are sometimes very important. The double dot in the rune for *ä*, for instance, has caused much perplexity.

Professor Magnus Olsen in his study of the Kingigtorsoak inscription discusses about thirty Greenland inscriptions, almost all from the fourteenth century. He points out a number of new runic forms,[14] which is also characteristic of the late inscriptions in the Scandinavian countries. The "golden age" of runic inscriptions was in the tenth and eleventh centuries when the art of writing runes became standardized. But by the end of the eleventh century Christianity had been generally introduced in the North, and the clergy frowned upon the use of runic writing because it was a doubtful legacy from heathendom. The use of runes became sporadic; there were no longer any masters in the art; the forms of many runes were forgotten; and new forms were added. In this respect the Kensington inscription is only a common example of its age—the fourteenth century.

This is well illustrated by Figure 8 which shows the gradual deterioration of the runic alphabet. Here the Kensington inscription shows nine new forms, and the Scanian Law which is a few years older also has nine new forms. The other two columns show runes from the seventeenth and eighteenth centuries, and they show a much greater corruption.

Summarizing this discussion, we have the following facts: On January 1, 1899, J. P. Hedberg, a businessman in Kensington,

Minn., wrote his letter to Mr. Turnblad, the editor of a Swedish newspaper in Minneapolis, in which he reports that a stone with an inscription had been found near Kensington. He enclosed a sheet of paper which he said was his exact copy of the inscription.

Ten years later, Mr. Hedberg requested the substance of this letter. In a letter to Professor Winchell, dated March 12, 1910, replying to an inquiry from the latter, Mr. Hedberg writes from Warroad, Minnesota:

> In the first place the stone was brought in to my office in Kensington by the finder Olof Ohman. I took quite much interest in the same. I copied the same and sent copy to S. J. Turnblad, who sent it to the State University but Prof. Breda thought it was a fake, in the Spring of 1890, I together with some others went out and did some digging where the stone had been found and will try and answer the following questions:
>
> 1 yes I saw the stump and roots.
> 2 the big root was grown as a bend and I am quite sure if we have had the stone there it would have fitted in it could not have grown on side of stone
> 3 as said large root run on top of stone
> 4 it is hard to say how old the tree was but it was quite large and must have been many years old any way a great deal older than the settlement there. I had quite atalk with one Nels Flaaten an old farmer that was along and helped Ohman to grub I considered him absolute reliable—he was along and grubbed the tree and dug out the stone and his statements confirmed absolutely with Ohmans. While I know very little about runes—I never considered the stone a fake.
>
> Very truly yours,
> J. P. HEDBERG[15]

Commenting on this letter, Wahlgren twice accuses Hedberg of being dishonest. He writes: "If Hedberg really did make the sketch . . . [he] was deliberately misleading Turnblad in 1899 when he pretended to think the runic symbols were 'old Greek letters.' "

"If, on the other hand, Hedberg merely accepted the sketch from Ohman . . . he was being untruthful eleven years later . . ."[16]

Why does Wahlgren mislead the public by saying that this old pioneer, Hedberg, was a liar? There is no evidence whatever that Hedberg was not telling the truth.

Wahlgren has a peculiar propensity for misrepresenting the facts. Referring to sketch map in one of the early reports on the finding of the stone, he writes: "One notices that a map reproduced with the sketch bears lettering in English: 'Slough,' 'Place where stone was found.' "[17] The natural conclusion of the reader is that the stone was found in the slough, which is one of Wahlgren's theories. But look at the sketch (Fig. 2)! Here we see that the finding place of the stone is properly marked with a cross, near the south-eastern corner of the sketch, while the word "slough" is a quarter mile away near the northern border of the sketch.[18]

chapter eleven

INTERNAL EVIDENCE OF
THE INSCRIPTION

There are only two alternative possibilities concerning the age of the Kensington inscription. One is that it was made after that part of Minnesota where it was found was settled by white people. If so, the inscription could be a fraud. But if its presence in its finding place antedates the arrival of the first white settlers, then it must be authentic since the Indians knew nothing about making runic inscriptions.

The circumstances of the discovery of the inscribed stone have been thoroughly investigated by the Minnesota Historical Society, the Norwegian Society of Minneapolis, and by many individuals. These investigations, with the exception of Wahlgren's, have all come to the same conclusion—namely that the stone with its face downward was found beneath a tree whose trunk was from eight to ten inches in diameter. In order to determine the age of this tree several trees of the same variety and size were cut down in the same vicinity, and cross sections of them were cut, dried and varnished. This made it possible to count the annual rings of growth. Olof Ohman, who found the stone, objected that these cross sections did not truly represent the age of the tree under which the stone was found because the latter was sickly and stunted, while the cross sections that were cut later were from healthy trees. However, to be on the safe side, it was decided to take the tree showing the *quickest growth* as an index to the age of the tree whose roots held the stone in a tight clasp. This quickest growing tree showed an age of forty-two years. The stone was therefore in its finding place at least as early as 1856. This was eleven years before the first pioneer reached the Kensington area, and the first wave of pioneers was still about one hundred miles away.

There is much other internal evidence which shows that the author of the inscription knew more about conditions and usage in the Scandinavian countries than any of his critics. Indications of this follow:

1. The inscription begins with a mention of the men in the party: eight Goths and twenty-two Norwegians. This mixture of two nationalities in one expedition has been a stumbling block to many. It was so for Helge Gjessing who was publicly called Professor Magnus Olsen's "best student" in the University of Oslo. In 1909 he was asked to write a paper on the Kensington Stone for discussion in the seminar. Gjessing did very well, but balked when he discussed the personnel of the expedition. He wrote: "The eight Goths do not in any circumstances fit in."

It was not only Gjessing who thought this was a gross error on the part of the runemaster, because Professor Olsen said that he (Olsen) and all the students in the seminar were in "full agreement" with Gjessing. This he wrote in a letter which he sent, with Gjessing's paper, to the editor of a quarterly in Decorah, Iowa.[1] Here we see that a university professor and his students in history were ignorant of the fact that a large part of West Gothland, including Dal, Wärmland, Lindholm Castle, Lödöse city, and many surrounding parishes continued to be parts of King Magnus' dominion after he had lost the Swedish crown and been rejected by the Swedes. The facts are these:

In 1335 when King Magnus married Blanche of Namur in Belgium, he gave his bride a wedding gift consisting of several large provinces in the southeastern part of Norway. These provinces comprised all of Borgesyssel, Ranrike, Marstrand and Bohuslen. He also gave her a number of districts in West Gothland and adjoining parts of Sweden. This was done with the approval of the Royal Council and his son Hakon who became king in 1355, and this made a third, compact little kingdom which was Magnus' and the queen's to rule to their death.[2]

Furthermore, King Magnus was personally a member of West Gothland's leading family (the Folkunga) and he was inclined to favor the people of this province, honoring many of them by appointment of their sons to his Royal Bodyguard which was the first big step to knighthood. In the 1350's when the Swedish aristocrats organized a revolt against the king, West Gothland was the only province which remained loyal to him. Because of this situation the people of West Gothland did not call themselves Swedes, but Goths, as on the Kensington Stone.

But if these facts were so obscure in 1909 that they were not known to leading scholars in the University of Oslo, how could a pioneer bush-whacker in Minnesota have known them?

2. There are also the numerals described in the preceding chapter. If it had not been for these numerals, it is probable that the inscription would have been given intelligent consideration. But none of the many Scandinavian professors in America had seen such numerals before and, like Professor Rygh in Oslo, they thought these numbers were an invention of the supposed "rune-faker" in Kensington.

It is not strange that these scholars did not know anything about the numerals because they are not discussed in any recent books about runes. The great period of runic inscriptions came to an end about 1250 when Christianity became dominant and the Latin alphabet came into general use. Our only information about them is to be found in Ole Worm's *Fasti Danici*, written and published in Latin in 1643, in which he describes a runic calendar of 1328, page 69. The imaginary runic forger of Kensington must therefore also have been familiar with Latin. But even this would have been of no help to him because I have corresponded with all the more important librarians of the Middle West and find that none of them had a copy of Ole Worm's book until many years after the Kensington inscription was found.

3. Another reminder of ancient usage which is now forgotten is the fact that the runemaster does not use miles or meters in reckoning distance, but so and so many *day voyages*. As G. M. Gathorne-Hardy, an expert on Norse voyages to America, says: "In the early days with which the present volume is concerned, the only method of measuring distances at sea was necessarily by time."[3] The average distance sailed in a twelve-

hour day became a standard unit of distance, and this, translated into English, was about seventy-five nautical miles. With this understanding of the meaning of a day-voyage, the distance mentioned in the inscription become perfectly clear. Then we read in the inscription that the sea where the ten men were left in charge of the ships was "14 *day-voyages*" north from "the island" where they left the inscribed stone. The nearest sea northward from Minnesota is Hudson Bay. As the distance from this "island" to Hudson Bay by way of Lake Winnipeg is 1050-1100 miles, this means that by a day's sailing or voyaging the runemaster meant a distance of about 75 nautical miles. This was considered an average day's sail and thus became a nautical unit of distance. Likewise, the runemaster says that the lake marked with two skerries, where the ten men were killed, was one *day-voyage to* the north. The distance between the finding place to the stone and the campsite at Cormorant Lake is about 75-80 miles. For shorter distances there was the *vika*, a distance of 6.25 nautical miles, or one-twelfth of a day-voyage.

But this method of reckoning distances became obsolete and was forgotten upon the introduction of steam-driven vessels. Because of this, no one knew the true meanings of these terms when the stone was found. The first to call attention to this old usage was Professor Wilhelm Hovgaard, who explains this medieval usage in his book, *Voyages of the Northmen to America,* 1914, 16 years *after* the stone was found. He was followed by Andrew Fossum in 1918 and Gathorne-Hardy in 1921. How, then, could any of the pioneers around Kensington have known about this method of reckoning distances in 1898 or earlier?

4. And how did this imaginary hoaxer up in Minnesota learn about the royal expedition to America? He would have to know of the king's commission to Paul Knutson back in 1354, its purpose, and its penetration to Hudson Bay. But the earliest information about this expedition was not made public until in 1888, when Gustav Storm's, *Studier over Vinlandsreiserne,* came out, and he says nothing about Hudson Bay.

5. The date on the stone, 1362, has been another puzzle for the critics. Some of them, like Wahlgren, in lieu of anything

better, have suggested that the runemaster must have been thinking of 1862, when the Sioux war broke out. But what has that to do with a voyage to America six hundred years ago? Now we are learning that there was an expedition, not only in America, but in Hudson Bay, in 1362! The first report of this enterprise did not appear until 1956.[4] At that time my knowledge of this new expedition was very limited, but in the next chapter of this book, I am happy to present a fairly complete report.

6. Professor Sven B. F. Janssen, the leading Swedish opponent of the Kensington inscription, claims that the prayer in the inscription, *A V M Save us from evil*, is impossible from a Catholic standpoint. He says: *"A Catholic would never think of addressing such a prayer to the Virgin Mary*, which at least shows that the carver was not a Catholic"* (the italics are his).[5]

Dr. Janssen here reflects the view which is common among people who are not Catholics that *Ave Maria* is not a prayer in the ordinary meaning, but a salutation or paean of praise. This idea is based on its beginning:

Hail Mary! Full of grace, the Lord is with thee;
Blessed art Thou among women and blessed is the fruit of thy womb, Jesus.

But this is only part of the Ave Maria. It continues with the following prayer:

Holy Mary, Mother of God, pray for us sinners, now and in the hour of our death.

The Latin text reads:

Sancta Maria, Mater Dei, ora pro nobis, nuncet in hora mortis nostrae. Amen.

This is the prayer which the distressed of all lands, yearning for her mother-love, made to the holy mother. It is also the prayer, repeated after every stanza, which we find in *Förnes-bronen*, the Telemark ballad from the middle of the fourteenth century:

Hjælpe oss Gud å Maria Möy
Å fælsæ oss alle av illy.
(Help us God and Virgin Mary
and save us all from evil)

We also find it in *Karlskrönikon*, a Swedish epic from 1452:[6]

Jomfra Maria, Gudz moder reen
beware Swerike fra alt meen.

In the inscription the A V M refers to the Ave Maria: "Holy Mary, Mother of God, pray for us sinners, now and in the hour of our death!" Then comes the "save us from evil," the most significant petition in Pater Noster. They were, and probably still are, the most popular prayers in the Catholic Church. Obviously, these two prayers in the inscription were not primarily inscribed for the benefit of the survivors—they were still in possession of their faculties and could make their own prayers. But not so with the ten dead men—their lips were silent. They had been stricken down suddenly without priestly atonement or extreme unction, and they were greatly in need of prayers. These two prayers in abbreviated form were therefore inscribed on the stone so that all who passed that way would read them and thus contribute toward the salvation of these unfortunates. This prayer for the dead may seem strange to Lutherans, but it is common among Catholics. Professor Morison, in his great work on Columbus, mentions a similar use of the same double appeal by an officer on Columbus' fourth voyage. On the stone above his grave is inscribed this epitaph: "Here lies the Honorable Gentleman, Diego Mendez," etc. *"He begs for Charity's sake a Pater Noster and an Ave Maria."*[7] A number of Catholic scholars have written with high approval of the true Catholic, medieval attitude of the inscription reflected by this double prayer.[8]

7. Professor Janssen also cites the sentence:

> (*vi*) *fan 10 man röde af blod og ded*
> ([vi] found 10 men red with blood and dead)

and insists that as the last word (*ded*) lacks inflection, it must have been written by a recent forger. But why should a modern person with his schooling and extensive reading be more apt to make a mistake in spelling than a person in the fourteenth century when there were no rules for spelling? The opposite seems more reasonable.

The fact is that there is not only one, but four mistakes here in the middle of the inscription. The runemaster did very well until he got down to the description of his ten dead companions. Then the mental vision of his bruised and crushed friends overpowers him and he makes four mistakes in describing the scene. First, he forgets the subject of the sentence (vi); second, he forgets that the word *döde* should be inflected like *röde*;[9] third, he spells this word with an *e* instead of *ö*; and fourth, he forgets the pronoun *os* in the prayer *fræelse* (*os*) *af illy*. This confused state of mind is understandable if we visualize the tragic situation. The writer of the inscription has here revealed some of his anguish.

8. The technique of the inscription shows that the letters were cut by a skilled craftsman who was as familiar with a chisel as an expert penman is with the pen. I have a letter dated March 20, 1960 from John K. Daniels, the Minnesota sculptor, in which he describes the style of the runemaster, as follows:

> Like many, I was a skeptic, largely because a neighbor assured me that he personally knew the man who had made the inscription. However, some years later I had the opportunity of closely examining the inscription in the museum of the Smithsonian Institution where it was on exhibition, and my skepticism left me. The indications were too clear in the manner in which the letters were cut that no modern joker would have carried out such a task, for no modern letterer would have done them as these were done. Whoever cut them was no novice, for the distribution of the letters is very good. The message itself, boiled down to our modern telegrammic brevity, is the strongest evidence in my opinion of its authenticity.

Many persons have been impressed by the solemn dignity of this inscription, but Wahlgren is not. He thinks the writer of

the inscription was trying to tell a funny story! But who except
Wahlgren can see anything funny in the brutal slaying of ten
men? He says the author of the inscription was a "waggish"
person who wrote a "whimsical inscription," filled with "amusing
ambiguities." The date is said to be "humorous," the carving
is "whimsical" and "done for fun." The "playful humor" of the
inscription is said to show that the runemaster had "a large sense
of humor," and the planting of the monument is called
"amusing"—all this and more is mentioned to show "the hoaxter"
(sic) was "a man of humor." This is Wahlgren's conception of
a great enterprise, inspired by brotherly love and seasoned with
the taste for adventure which is one of the accompaniments of
exploration. Their course led over heaving seas and through
vast wildernesses—a truly great conquest of man!

chapter twelve

A FORGOTTEN EXPLORER

The name of Nicholas of Lynn is not known to the general public. In fact, he is so little known that even the big encyclopedias have no information about him. Yet Nicholas was the first of England's long line of explorers, and he performed an outstanding deed. He discovered Hudson Bay 250 years before Henry Hudson's visit, and he was the first to determine the approximate location of the Magnetic Pole. He wrote a book about his travels, but as this was many years before the printing press was invented, this book is now lost. However, it was known to some cartographers, and they say that Nicholas spent two years or so in Hudson Bay around 1360. They also say that he was a member of an expedition which divided into two parts, which gave him time and opportunity to make his explorations. He returned to Bergen, Norway, in 1363 or 1364 with seven survivors and then went back to England.

In the Kensington inscription we learn that the royal expedition sent out by King Magnus was also in Hudson Bay at this very time. The Kensington inscription further mentions that its expedition divided after reaching Hudson Bay, twenty men going inland, while ten men remained to guard the ship. As this was a most unlikely time for an expedition to America, and as both of these expeditions divided in two and then returned to Europe in 1363 or 1364, the question arises: Do these reports deal with the one and same expedition?

It may also be asked: Are the reports about these two expeditions dependable?

As far as the Kensington inscription goes, it is still on trial. We have historical evidence, preserved in Norwegian documents, that such an expedition was planned and dispatched, and that the survivors returned to Norway in 1363 or 1364 (see chapter II above). About Nicholas of Lynn there has been no debate because very little is known about him. It is therefore necessary to inquire if such a man ever existed; and, if so, what did he do?

From various sources we learn that there was a Franciscan or Carmelite friar or Minorite who was called Nicholas of Lynn (King's Lynn, Norfolk). He is said to have been a good mathematician who invented or developed the nautical instrument called an astrolabe. This made it possible to determine the latitude of any place where the observation could be taken with reasonable accuracy. He made an astrolabe for Prince John, Duke of Lancaster, who was the principal patron of the arts and sciences in his day. Because of this gift, Nicholas was called The Man with the Astrolabe.

About 1364 he wrote a small book entitled *De Inventione Fortunata* (The Fortunate Discovery). In this he tells of a voyage to an inland ocean, far north, which he called *Mare Sugenum* (Sucking Sea) which, if the narrative is true, can only have been Hudson Bay.

The earliest surviving mention of this book is an annotation on the map of the cartographer, Johan Ruysch, dated 1508 (see Fig. 14). He writes:

> We read in the book *De Inventione Fortunata* that beneath the Arctic Pole there is a high rock of magnetic stone, thirty-three German miles in circumference.
>
> The *Mare Sugenum* surrounds this rock, flowing as if through a funnel [that is, like a whirlpool].
>
> There are four islands of which two are inhabited. They are bordered by mountains twenty-four days' journey across, which forbid human habitation.
>
> Here the *Mare Sugenum* begins. Here the ship's compass does not hold, nor can ships containing iron turn back.

According to Ruysch's summary, Nicholas did not locate the Magnetic Pole at the geographical pole—as everyone thought and continued to think he had done—but below it. Ruysch's accompanying map shows the *Mare Sugenum* lying more than a thousand miles from the pole (see Fig. 14).

Another writer who is said to have seen Nicholas' book was Ferdinand Columbus who says that one of the things which encouraged his father was the mention in *Inventione Fortunata* of islands in the West.¹ Bartolome de Las Casas also mentions Nicholas' book.²

There was another man who must be mentioned because his reading of Nicholas' *Inventione Fortunata* resulted in a great improvement of the cartography of his times. He was Claudius Clavus, a Dane, born in 1388. Early in the following century he made a map of Europe which at first was scorned by the scholars of his times because it violated the then accepted geographical conclusions. However, Cardinal Fillastre, a liberal-minded man, made a copy of the original in 1427 and this is still preserved.

Up to the time of Clavus and long afterward the most generally accepted theory of the earth was that it was a round disk, around which flowed the vast outer sea. In the center of this disk was placed Jerusalem. The disk was divided into two halves by a line running north and south. The eastern or right hand half was Asia. The western half was further divided by a line running east and west, representing the Mediterranean; the northern quarter was Europe, the southern quarter was Africa. Maps showing the above details are called wheel-maps because the bisecting lines are suggestive of a wagon wheel, and this type of map was held in high regard for almost a thousand years as being a plain and true picture of the earth's position and nature.

As long as men stayed at home, this cosmography seemed adequate and proper. But when they became curious and sailed far out on the outer sea, discovering new islands and even a continent, serious problems arose because the maps did not provide room for any such ventures. The first historian to be confronted by this problem was Adam of Bremen when he wrote his great history of the Hamburg diosese (1073) which then embraced all of northern Europe. He interviewed all whom he thought could give him information, among them King Swen of Denmark. The king astounded Adam by telling him of large islands far out in the outer sea and of a country called Wineland, several thousand miles away, where luscious grapes grew in abundance. This was entirely at variance with what Adam had been taught, but, on the other hand, the king was a great and well-informed man. He therefore tells it all with the exception of the reported location of these new lands. They could not lie far out west in the outer sea—such an idea was almost blasphemous! Instead he describes them as lying north of Norway where they were still within the earth's limits! This was found to be a good way to preserve respect for the time-honored concept, and Greenland continued to be placed north and northeast of Norway.[3]

But then came Clavus with his complete defiance of venerated dogma. He not only said that Greenland lay a couple of thousand miles out *west*, he also claimed that it was a huge land more than a thousand miles long. Furthermore, he said it was shaped like a wedge with its pointed end to the south and said that the latitude of this southern point was 59° 15′—an observation so close to verity that it lacks only a half degree of being scientifically correct. These facts, now well known, prove that Clavus must have visited Greenland or obtained his information from one who had been there. Clavus did in fact claim that he had visited Greenland, but commentators agree that this is a lie. He said that he had seen the Eskimo in great armies marching down from the northern parts—Eskimos knew nothing about army warfare. He also says he had visited a cloister—St. Thomas—on the 75th parallel which was heated by hot springs. It is true that there are hot springs in Greenland. But they are close to the south end, and no St. Thomas is on record in Greenland. And there are other errors. Finally, the man who took the latitude observations was a navigator and had the necessary instruments, which probably were not known to Clavus. As will be shown later, Nicholas of Lynn was in Greenland in 1363, and Clavus must have obtained his information about Greenland from Nicholas' book.[4]

But while it can be shown that Nicholas of Lynn was in Greenland in the latter half of the fourteenth century, we have not yet presented any evidence that he also visited Hudson Bay. Fortunately, it happens that the reports about his *Mare Sugenum* (The Sucking Sea) mention many physiographic details. If these descriptions agreed with what is now known about Hudson Bay, this question would be definitely settled. A course of reading everything that has been written about the physiography of Hudson Bay seemed necessary.

But the material proved disappointing. The big encyclopedias, both foreign and domestic, have very little information about Hudson Bay. While many scientific expeditions have been sent there, they were all interested only in the geology or ornithology of the Bay, or the Northwest Passage, and Nicholas does not mention any of these things. The problem remained unsolved for several years.

However, in 1957, the Canadian Hydrographic Service put on sale its first *Coast Pilot* dealing with navigation on Hudson Bay, and I obtained a copy. In it is found a full description of all its islands, currents, whirlpools, magnetic disturbances, etc., and these are the things that Nicholas dwells on. Let us now see if Nicholas' descriptions agree with those of the *Coast Pilot*. First comes the location.

1. Nicholas lived in the middle of the fourteenth century. Prior to his alleged voyage no one knew anything about any inland sea in America.

Nor was there any additional knowledge about the interior of North America 150 years later when Johan Ruysch in 1508 made his map of subarctic America, based on Nicholas' book. Ruysch by this map quotes Nicholas as saying that a mountainous region (*Berga extrema*) lay west of Greenland. West of that lay the *Mare Sugenum* and its four islands with their fearful currents (see Figure 14).

This is as correct as can be shown on a small sketch. West of Greenland lies sterile Labrador with its towering mountains, and west of this lies Hudson Bay with the four troublesome islands right in the opening.

2. Captain George Best, a member of the Frobisher expedition of 1576, wrote the following description of Nicholas' indrawing sea: "As Mercator mentionet out of a probable author, there was a frier of Oxford who himselfe went verrye farre north above 200 years ago. . . . He reporteth that the southwest

parte of that lande is a fruitfull and holesome soyle. The northeast parte is inhabited by a people called pygmei, which are
not at the uttermost above four foote highe. . . ."[5]

To understand this description, it must be remembered
that Nicholas had no other opportunity of observing the land
around the sea than that of inspecting it from the deck of his
ship or at a camp on the shore. He did not travel by land and
knew nothing about the interior. Nor did anyone else. When
he says that the land on the southwest had a fruitful soil, he
could only mean the land on the southwest side of the sea on
which he was sailing. Similarly, the pygmies that he saw were
presumably on Baffin Land northeast of him. This is precisely
true. There is no "fruitful soil" on the *west* side of Hudson Bay
—only the bleak tundra. The Bay has no south side and only
bare rock on the east. But on the southwest side is a forest at
least two hundred miles wide. To the northeast lies Baffin Land,
favored by the Eskimo.

Captain Luke Foxe, who in 1631 spent the entire summer
in following the southwest coast of Hudson Bay, describes it
thus: "The land gently descends to the seaside, the greenest and
best since I came out of the river Thames, and it was enclosed
with thick rows of trees between one meadow and another." He
says that the banks of the Nelson River were full of timber. Of
the timber he says: "It is the best fir that I have seen and I do
think the best in the world."[6] On shore he found "good grass,
blackberries, strawberries, gooseberries and several sorts of
shrubs."

3. James Cnoyen, who claims that he obtained his information directly from Nicholas' shipmates in 1364, says he was told
that in this sea were many channels or currents. He says "They
are called indrawing seas because the current always flows northward so strongly that no wind can make a ship sail back against
it."[7]

The reason for this continuous northward current is the
fact that Hudson Bay is the drainage basin for almost one-fourth
of the whole North American continent. A letter to me from the
Canadian Department of Northern Affairs, dated February 17,
1960, reports that the St. Lawrence River discharges about

3,750,000 gallons per second. The Hudson Bay watershed is vastly larger, and as nearly all its rivers empty into its southern half, this causes a constant flow northward.

4. Most of the quotations from or about Nicholas dwell on the many strong currents in the *Mare Sugenum*. Captain George Best who in his book, *True Discourse*, published in 1578, shows himself well informed for that period, quotes Mercator's description of the sea visited by the author of *Inventio Fortunata*. He says "it is divided into four partes or Ilandes by foure greate guttes, indrafts, or channels, running violently, and delivering themselves into a monstrous receptacle and swallowing sincke, with such a violent force and current, that a shippe beyng entred never so little within one of these foure indrafts, cannot be holden backe by the force of any great winde, but runneth in headlong by that deep swallowing, into the bowels of the earth."[8]

In the northeast corner of Hudson Bay, where its waters meet the waters of Fox Channel and Hudson Strait, lie four large islands which are constantly pounded by the swift currents of these opposing waters. These are the two Mill Islands and Salisbury and Nottingham. The two Mill Islands were so named by William Baffin because of the great grinding of the ice in that vicinity. Captain Baffin explored this part of Hudson Bay in 1615 and writes:

> The ilands or iles, lying in the middle of the channell, hauinge many sounds runninge through them, with dyuers points and headlands, encountering the force of the tyde, caused such a rebounde of water and ice *that unto them that saw it not is almost incredible. But our ship being thus in the partition between the eddy which runne one waye, and the stream which runne another, endured so great an extremytie, that unless the Lord himselfe had beene on our side we had shurely perished; for somtymes the ship was hoysed aloft; and at other tymes shee hauinge, as it were, got the uepper hand, would force greate mighty peeces of ice to sinke downe on the side of her, and rise on the other.* [The italics are his].

Captain Baffin made a good map of this part of Hudson Bay, showing the four islands, Nottingham, Salisbury, and the two Mill Islands.[9] These four islands lie just where the waters of Hudson Bay, Fox Channel and Hudson Strait meet.

Mr. G. P. Putnam, director of the Putnam expedition in 1937, in an article in the *Geographical Review,* in which he describes the northeastern part of Hudson Bay, wrote: "The fabulously swift tidal currents with their propensity for grinding the ice and swirling it fearsomely hither and yon, are as startling today as then," [that is, in Baffin's day].[10] The excessive turbulence of this area is emphasized by nearly all later explorers.

5. Nicholas is quoted by Mercator, Heylin and Best as saying that this sea drains into a gulf with many whirlpools, so difficult to navigate that sailing vessels caught in them cannot get away.

This is a good description of Hudson Strait through which the waters of Hudson Bay reach the Atlantic. The strait has a tide of 35 feet—even 52 feet has been recorded in *the Hudson Bay Coast Pilot*—and when this meets the currents from Hudson Bay and Fox Channel, the problem of navigating a sailing vessel becomes very serious. If in addition the wind is blowing, the situation becomes desperate.

6. Mercator quotes Cnoyen as saying that "there is never in those parts so much wind as might be sufficient to drive a cornmill."[11]

This is an exaggeration, but the quietness of the atmosphere has been noted by many. *The New International Encyclopedia* says: "Hudson Bay is singularly free from storm and fog."

7. Cnoyen was also informed that the Minorite, that is, Nicholas, said that large parts of the "indrawing sea" did not freeze over in winter."[12]

This is also true of Hudson Bay which is the only body of water west of Greenland which in its greater part is open in winter. The *Coast Pilot*, p. 13, says that the ice in winter "extends off the coast shore for 60 or 70 miles to include the islands, and the remainder of the bay from one to five miles."

8. Johan Ruysch, quoting *Inventione Fortunata,* on the margin of his map of 1508, says that in the *Mare Sugenum,* "Here the ships compass does not hold, nor can ships that carry iron cannot turn back."

The Hudson Bay Coast Pilot (pages 14 and 263) says that

there is so much magnetic disturbance in the northern part of Hudson Bay that "the magnetic compass cannot be relied upon in the approach to Churchill Harbor (on the west coast) in consequence of this magnetic disturbance."

9. Ruysch also quotes Nicholas as saying that below the arctic pole is "a high mountain of magnetic rock, 33 leagues in circumference, the land adjoining being torn by the sea into four islands."[13]

The map accompanying the *Hudson Bay Coast Pilot* shows that just west of the four big islands (see point 4 above) stands Mount Minto, a towering rock almost 1,100 feet high and in plain view of them. It is now known to be an appendage to Southampton Island, but, according to the *Coast Pilot* (p. 266), was formerly thought to be a separate island. It lies close to the area where, according to the *Coast Pilot*, "the compass cannot be relied upon."

10. Ruysch, quoting Nicholas says that the sea around these four islands is "bounded by huge mountains." This is correct. On the east side northern Labrador is flanked by a wall of naked cliffs from a thousand to six thousand feet high. On the north is the mountainous Baffin land, and on the west is the northeastern coast of Southampton Island, 200 miles long, rising from 1,000 to 1,500 feet high.

With these many points of identification, there can be no doubt about Nicholas' voyage to Hudson Bay. Only after personal inspection would it be possible to describe the many physical circumstances of Hudson Bay as closely as he has done.[14]

There is another probable proof of Nicholas' sojourn in Hudson Bay. About fifty years ago a globe of the world was found in Zerbst, Anhalt, Germany. It was made about 1537 by Gemma Frisius, one of the best cartographers in the sixteenth century, and is reproduced in part in 1911 in A. A. Björnbo's *Cartographia Groenlandica*.[15] This globe shows a good map of Hudson Bay (see Fig. 15). In the north we see the opening to Fox Channel and in the south is James Bay, somewhat too large. In the northeast we see the opening to Hudson Strait. The west coast is almost perfect, with Chesterfield Inlet, Churchill River and the Nelson, all shown in their proper places. The Nelson and the Hayes have a joint outlet and this is also shown. It might be objected that this inland sea is pictured as lying in Asia, but this is due to the then reigning conclusion that Greenland was a part of Asia.

But possibly the critics will object: How would it be possible for Nicholas to make a voyage to America in the 1360's? An exploration of several years' duration would cost a lot of money, and Nicholas, a mendicant monk, certainly had none. Nor was the English government interested. Aside from John Cabot's voyage in 1497, it was more than two hundred years before the English became interested in America.

This is quite true. The great age of exploration was still more than a hundred years away, and Prince Henry the Navigator was not yet born. A voyage by the English to America at this time seems quite inconceivable, being without a reasonable motive.

But the situation was quite different when we consider the circumstances in Greenland. There, in the western colony, the people had been harassed so much that they had decided, like their ancestors who had settled in Greenland, to seek homes elsewhere. This was a crown colony, but the king had forgotten them. Too late, the king realized that through his neglect he had endangered the salvation of these poor people, and in deep self-reproach he gave orders to the Commandant, Paul Knutson, to go and find these people and bring them back to the arms of the Church, as related in Chapter II of this book.

But is it likely that an Englishman would be a member of a Swedish-Norwegian expedition?

The knowledge of geography in the Middle Ages was so scant that all countries interested in exploration were glad to avail themselves of foreign experts. Spain's greatest progress was made by help of three foreign navigators—Columbus, Vespucci, and Magellan. The first French voyage to America was guided by Verrazano, a Florentine, and the first English vessel sent into the West was commanded by John Cabot, a Venetian. Lynn in Norfolk, England, was the principal port of Norwegian trade in England, and many Norwegians lived there.[16] There was

therefore brisk intercourse between Lynn and Bergen, from
which port the royal expedition sailed. Moreover, Gisbrikt, the
Bishop of Bergen at that time, was an Englishman, and he was
probably deeply interested in the success of this great religious
crusade to an unknown country. He would therefore urge upon
the commandant, who also lived in Bergen, the wisdom of
securing the services of his famous countryman, The Man with
the Astrolabe.

We have four reports, all of which deal with a voyage to
America in the early 1360's.

The FIRST is the historical information about the cause
and purpose of a royal expedition, sent to Greenland and the
west, as set forth by Gustav Storm[17] and repeated by me in
Chapter II of this book. According to Storm, the survivors
returned to Norway in 1363 or 1364.

The SECOND is the report of Nicholas of Lynn, the date
when he reached Hudson Bay, his description of it, the division
of the expedition in 1362, and his return to Norway a year or
two later.

The THIRD is the Kensington inscription which also tells
of the division of the expedition at Hudson Bay and what later
befell the men who went inland in 1362.

The FOURTH is the report of Jacob Cnoyen, a Hollander,
who in 1364 visited Bergen, Norway, and there talked with the
survivors of the group who had been with Nicholas of Lynn on
his great voyage. Cnoyen wrote a lengthy report about Nicholas
which two hundred years later came to the attention of Gerard
Mercator, the great cartographer, who had borrowed Cnoyen's
original report. He told his friend, John Dee, about Cnoyen's
report, and the latter was eager to see it. Being unable to get
the original report again, Mercator made a lengthy synopsis of
it from memory and gave it to his friend. This synopsis was
later deposited in the British Museum which upon request
kindly sent me a photostat copy in 1955. It is written partly in
Dutch and partly in Latin and has been exposed to fire, for
many of the pages have scorched edges. However, much of the
manuscript is still legible. It was translated by Professor E. G. R.

Taylor (London) and printed in *Imago Mundi* in 1956. Below are a number of quotations from Cnoyen, the first being inscribed on the margin of Mercator's world map of 1569.

> Touching the description of the North partes, I have taken the same out of the voyage of James Cnoyen of Hartzevan Buske. . . . The most part, and the chiefest things among the rest, he (Cnoyen) learned of a certaine priest in the King of Norwayes Court, in the year 1364. This priest [Ivar Bardsson] was descended from them which King Arthur had sent to inhabit these Islands, and he reported that in the yeare 1360, a certain English Frier, a Franciscan, and Mathematician of Oxford, came into those Islands, who leaving them, and passing further by his Magical Arte, described all those places that he sawe, and took the height of them with his Astrolabe. . . .

Cnoyen's report on his interviews with Ivar Bardson and the survivors of Nicholas of Lynn's division of the expedition would probably have been most helpful if John Dee had left it as originally transcribed by Mercator. But Dee was seeking royal favor by claiming that the mythical King Arthur about 530 had conquered and peopled Iceland and Greenland which, he claimed, rightfully belonged to England. These false claims he clumsily inserted into Cnoyen's report at various points with the hope that it would bring him both honor and riches. In his diary of November 28, 1577, he wrote: "I declared to the queen her title to Greenland etc. Estotiland, Friseland,"[18] and, quite likely, the queen gave him a gracious smile. But Lord Burghley who controlled the purse was not interested in fairy tales, and it all came to naught.

The following is John Dee's summary of Cnoyen's report:

> Anno 1360 . . . a friar of Oxford, being a good astronomer went in company with others to the most Northern Islands of the world and there, leaving his company together, he travailed alone, and purposely described all the Northern Islands with the indrawing seas; and the record thereof he, at his return, delivered to the King of England. The name of which book is Inventio Fortunata, which book begins at

54° and goes as far as the pole. Which friar has since journed to and fro for the King of England on business.[19]

If we look upon the Nicholas expedition as a separate voyage, it is difficult to see what could have been its purpose. This was hundreds of years before there was any interest in a possible Northwest Passage or the search for the North Pole. What could have prompted him to sail up into the Arctic and linger there for two years? And why did his expedition split up in two parts? There seems to be no sense in this. But if he were a part of the expedition simultaneously sent out by King Magnus, then we find an intelligent purpose in it all.

That expedition was sent out to find a group of Norsemen who were said to have given up the Christian faith and emigrated to some unknown place beyond Greenland. We do not know when it sailed from Norway, but it was some time after 1354. On arriving in America, its first purpose would be to build a fortified base of operations. This would probably be in Vinland, so named because of its abundance of grapes. In fact, the Kensington inscription says the expedition came from Vinland. There is reason to believe that the headquarters were at present Newport in Rhode Island.

The only course that promised any success was to carefully search the shore for signs of the lost Greenlanders. As these people were accustomed to a cool climate, this search would be mainly northward. The first location mentioned by Nicholas, as recorded by Cnoyen, is a spot on the coast of Labrador at latitude 54. The date he gives is 1360. This may mean that this point was the starting point on the northward search. But as most of the sheets of the Cnoyen narrative have been damaged on the right side, several other latitudinal points may have been obliterated. This possibility is supported by the fact that this observation was made as late as 1360. In all events this location is highly significant because latitude 54 enters Labrador at Hamilton Inlet, the most probable location for new homes of the lost Greenlanders. This inlet and its big appendage, Lake Melville, extends westward for about two hundred miles with an abundance of good fishing and hunting grounds and a wealth of timber for housebuilding and fuel. Nowhere along the entire coastline is there a more promising place for the home-seeking Greenlanders. As it would take many weeks for the search party to inspect this large area, a winter camp was probably made here, which would give Nicholas many opportunities for using his astrolabe.

Northward from Hamilton Inlet the coast of Labrador and Hudson Strait is stern and forbidding, and the travelers would find little or no place suitable for settlement by the Greenlanders. But on reaching Cape Wolstenholm, they were pleasantly surprised to find the coast making an abrupt turn to the south. For nine hundred miles their course was now straight south, and they may have thought they were circumnavigating a vast peninsula which would lead them to the people they were seeking. But when they reached the mud flats of James Bay, they saw the coast turn west. Still hopeful, they turned west and and followed it to Nelson River. But here the coast turned north again into the Arctic waste. The open season of 1361 was now coming to an end. Here they built their winter camp.[20]

The next spring the members of the expedition made an important decision. They decided that further search for the Greenlanders was useless. Those poor people had probably perished. The next thing was to return home or to their headquarters in Vinland. But there were two ways to go home. One was to return the way they had come, and that route did not appeal to most of them. The other was to go overland by help of the rivers and lakes. Twenty men out of the total of thirty voted for that. As it would not be wise to close the door for a possible return by sea, ten men including Nicholas of Lynn were left in charge of the two boats. They were no doubt instructed to remain there for a year before starting on their homeward voyage. This explains how it happened that Nicholas had time to make the explorations he describes.

As the twenty men who went inland did not return, Nicholas in 1363 sailed for Greenland. Two men had died during the year of waiting, so there were only eight survivors including himself. On the way along the coast of Greenland he was attacked by Eskimos, but beat them back and captured two of their kayaks as mentioned previously. Ivar Bardsson, the steward of all the episcopal properties, was no doubt very happy to see Nicholas because Ivar had been marooned on Greenland for fourteen years. He was very anxious to return to Norway so he could report the death of the Greenland bishop in 1349. The following are some of the communications made by Nicholas to Ivar Bardson, who in turn mentioned them to Jacob Cnoyen:

> Anno Domini 1364 came eight of these persons to Norway to the King. Among them were two clerics. One of them had an astrolabe who in the fifth generation was descended from a Brusselite. These eight were of the original party who had penetrated the Northern Regions.[21]

On the next page there is a similar but somewhat different statement. He writes:

> The priest who had the astrolabe told the King of Norway that a Minorite from Oxford who was a good astronomer had come into these northern islands in 1360. He separated from the others who had come . . . and wrote about all the remarkable things among the islands in a book which he gave to the King of England which he in Latin called Inventio Fortunatae. This book begins at the last climate, that is to say from latitude 54, and goes to the pole.[22]

Here we find that while the astrolabe was first exhibited by Nicholas, it later came into the possession of Ivar Bardsson in exchange for a testament. Cnoyen says that when Nicholas left Norway, he gave the astrolabe to his seven shipmates who in turn gave it to Ivar Bardsson. We know that he arrived in Bergen in 1363 or 1364 because he was then appointed Canon of the Church of the Apostles in Bergen. This was the most important of the fourteen royal chapels. As his appointment is dated June 25, 1364,[23] it is probable that he arrived in Bergen late the preceding fall because the drift ice usually keeps the harbors of Greenland closed until August 1 or later.

The most amazing thing about this group of explorers was their decision to return to their headquarters in Vinland by an

overland journey. Twenty men set out on this venture leaving
ten men to take care of their vessels.

Why did they undertake such an excessively risky venture?
There may have been two or three reasons. They had come so
far north, then west, then south, that they may have thought
that they had traveled around three sides of a huge quadrangle,
leaving only the fourth side to be travelled. But this is doubtful
because they had no sure way to estimate the length of the
inland voyage.

A more probable reason is that all of them must have heard
about Marco Polo's great journey to China. There, far beyond
the deserts and mountains of Asia, he had found a land and
people of great riches, and the story of his adventures was known
in every European court. Surely God had not created this new
continent in vain! If not, then they were on the threshold of a
land of great opportunities, and they would be simpletons not
to explore it. As this expedition consisted partly of members of
the King's Bodyguard and partly of other men who had been
carefully chosen for their mental and physical excellence, this
group was perhaps as fit for their enterprise as any who came
to America in its early days.

Much has been said about the impossibility of ascending the
Nelson River. This criticism is based on ignorance and is fully
answered in Chapter V of this book. Above the Nelson is Lake
Winnipeg, about three hundred miles long, and here they no
doubt made good time. At the south end of this lake, they came
to Red River, a large waterway running due north and south.

They apparently met with no adventure worth mentioning
until they reached Cormorant Lake in Becker Country, about a
thousand miles from Hudson Bay. Here they appear to have
been short of food because no less than ten men went out to
fish. This was a grave mistake, for upon returning they found
their ten comrades "red with blood and dead."

While this was a most grievous blow, it did not deter the ten
survivors from continuing their voyage south and east for almost
a hundred miles to the former lake on Ohman's farm. Here
they found a stone suitable for an inscription. This inscription
is a masterpiece in several respects, showing that the one who

made it was an expert in the use of the chisel. The author of the inscription was probably a man of literary skill because he tells the first great story from America's earliest past in very few words, including a double prayer. Such was and is his legacy.

With the above facts before us, we can now make the following summary:

1. The Kensington Stone tells of a voyage to America in or about 1360. The other three reports do likewise.

2. Three of the four narratives tell of visiting Hudson Bay in 1362.

3. After arriving there, the Kensington Stone says that the expedition divided in two parts. The Nicholas narrative and Cnoyen's mention a similiar division.

4. According to the Kensington inscription, this took place in 1362. The Nicholas report does not mention the year, but as shown above and below, it must have been in 1362.

5. The Kensington Stone says that ten men were left with the ships. Nicholas says nothing about how many men were left behind, but when he in 1363 returned to Greenland, he brought seven men back besides himself. Two had perished.

6. The Kensington inscription is a record of a Norse expedition. Nicholas' men were also Norse, because his seven survivors all returned to Norway, not England.

7. Professor Storm says the royal expedition returned in 1363 or 1364. Nicholas also returned to Norway in 1363 or 1364.

But what happened to the large contingent who remained at the headquarters in Vinland? That will be touched upon in a later chapter.

chapter thirteen

STONES THAT SPEAK

It is well known that Minnesota has a runic inscription. In translated form it contains almost a hundred words and is one of the longest of all inscriptions in stone or wood.

But it is not well known that Minnesota has twelve other stones, all of which repeat the same brief but significant message: *"Here we were and spent the night."*

These thirteen stones contain no words in any language, but they nonetheless testify to the presence of a group of determined men with steel tools, traveling in a large boat, and speaking of campsites and a well-defined route of travel from Lake Winnipeg to the center of Minnesota. They are mooring stones, marking more than a dozen campsites. There are also two campsites otherwise marked.

A mooring stone is a boulder or ledge of rock on the shore of a lake or body of water which was made to serve as a pier for boats. To make it serviceable, a hole was drilled in the upper surface of the boulder for the reception of a ringbolt or iron pin. With one end of the boat anchored in deep water and the other end tied to this improvised pier, the boat lay safe even if a strong wind was blowing.

Up to 1919 there was no knowledge about mooring stones in America. That came about through the search for the camp where ten of the explorers of 1362 were killed, as stated in the inscription on the Kensington Stone. This is described as follows:

We had our camp by two skerries one day-voyage north from this stone. We were out and fished one day. When we returned we found 10 men red with blood and dead. Ave Maria! Save us from evil!

As a skerry is an outcrop of the underlying bedrock and is surrounded by water, this can only mean that the camp was on the shore of a lake marked by two such bare outcrops. Assuming that a day's travel was from fifteen to thirty miles in length, all the lakes within that distance lying north from the finding place of the stone were inspected for skerries, but in vain.

It was finally discovered that the difficulty was not in the inscription but in our ignorance of old-time usage. This was made clear by William Hovgaard, Professor of Navigation at the Massachusetts Institute of Technology. In 1915 he published a book on the *Voyage of the Northmen to America*. In this book he shows that the term *day voyage* or *day sailing* was a unit of distance equal to about seventy-five nautical miles. This was based on the fact that an average twelve-hour's sailing with a fair wind covered this distance. Shortly afterward, Professor A. Fossum of St. Olaf College[1] and G. M. Gathorne-Hardy of London[2] reached the same conclusion.

As Hovgaard's interpretation of *day voyage* is clear and convincing, I immediately set out on another search for the lake with the two skerries. This lake must have been quite large as the men who went fishing apparently did not see or hear anything of the massacre of their friends. The map of Minnesota shows that about seventy-five nautical miles north of the finding place of the stone are many lakes, some quite large. The largest of these is Cormorant Lake in Becker County, about five miles long and almost half as wide. Here I decided to begin my search. The nearest railway station was Audubon, and here I arrived early one Sunday morning after an all-night ride in a day coach.

I looked about to seek information about what road to take to get to Cormorant Lake. Audubon was a very small village. There was a small general store and a blacksmith shop, both of which were closed, the day being Sunday. There was also a church, a parsonage and a couple of cottages. The latter had drawn window curtains, but in the parsonage life was going on as usual, and the parson came out to meet me as I approached the house. He was very accommodating and said he would take me within two miles of Cormorant Lake as he had services in that neighborhood that morning. In the meantime he invited me to come in and have breakfast.

It was good to have a hearty breakfast after my long vigil on the train, and it was also good to sit in the parson's buggy. After a ride of about an hour we came to a crossroad. Here the parson stopped: "Now if you will turn west here, you will see the lake a couple of miles away. Meanwhile I go east to my congregation. Good luck!"

After a half hour's walk, I saw the lake in the distance. It was rough country with many steep hills and wet marshes. Only now and then did I get a glimpse of the lake, but saw no skerry.

At the northwest corner of the lake was a very high and steep hill, rising from the shore of the lake. It promised to give a wide view, and with much anticipation I climbed up. It was indeed a fine view because now I saw the whole lake sparkling in the morning sun. And—best of all—there I saw two skerries! One was only about a quarter mile away, and the other, in direct line with the former, was perhaps two miles away. I followed the shore southward, but only from the high point mentioned above could both skerries be seen at once.

Were these the two skerries that the runemaster had seen six hundred years ago, or were there other lakes similarly marked? Erik Wahlgren in California is sure that the Minnesota lakes are crowded with skerries. He says: "Endless rocky islets —the definition of skerry—can be found here."[3]

The above emphatic statement shows that he knows practically nothing about the lake region of Minnesota. A skerry is an outcropping of the original bedrock, and this bedrock in Minnesota was deeply covered by glacial drift. This is definitely stated by Professor George A. Thiel, Chairman of the Department of Geology and Mineralogy at the University of Minnesota. He writes:

I have your letter of May 16, requesting information in regard to rocks in the lake region of Minnesota between Detroit Lakes and Glenwood. . . .

In the area to which you refer the glacial drift is very thick and consequently there are no outcrops of solid bedrock in that entire area.[4]

Even the two skerries mentioned above are not true skerries, but are two very small heaps of coarse gravel which at a distance look exactly like true skerries. They are the only formations of their kind in this region, as I verified by a careful inspection of all the lakes lying from seventy-five to one hundred miles north of the finding place of the inscribed stone near Kensington.

Some time later in the same year, 1919, I gave a talk in a church near Cormorant Lake and told of the discovery of the two skerries. This interested my audience so much that I was asked to go with them to Cormorant Lake and show them the skerries. The next morning a group of twenty-five or thirty men went with me. After viewing the skerries from the big hill mentioned above, we all went down to the shore of the lake. Here we saw a pile of big stones on the beach almost hidden by the thick underbrush, and someone discovered that a hole about an inch in diameter and about seven inches deep had been chiseled in the top of one of the big boulders. A straight stick was found and when that was placed in the hole, it was found that the axis of the hole was not truly vertical but inclined slightly toward the lake. The inside of the hole was as smooth as glass.

What did this mean? As the Indians had no tools for boring deep holes in a granite boulder, it must have been made by a white man, but what was his purpose? It was not done to make way for the plow because no farming is done on the beach. Nor was it done to obtain building stone. In the Lake Park region there is an abundance of small stones suitable for building a foundation, but this was rarely done by the pioneers because they built their log houses right on the bare ground.

The significance of this hole in the boulder remained a mystery for many years and was increased from time to time by the discovery of other boulders in different places with similar holes.

However, that mystery came to an end when I obtained a copy of Archbishop Olaus Magnus' great work, *Historia de Gentibus Septentrionalibus.* He lost his office when the Protestant revolution upset the supremacy of the Roman Catholic Church in the first half of the sixteenth century. However, he spent his time well and wrote his great descriptive and cultural history of Sweden and other northern countries. This work was printed in 1555. In this history he also describes and pictures how the people in the north secured their vessels on the rockbound shore by drilling a hole in the top of a boulder into which a ringbolt was fixed.[5] The Swedish historian, Professor C. G. Styffe, shows that this was done even thousands of years ago,[6] and when I visited the west coast of Norway in 1928, I found these improvised piers were still in use.

We have now found thirteen of these mooring stones; one being on an island in Berens River Harbor on Lake Winnipeg, and twelve in northwestern Minnesota (see Figure 13). In each case inquiry was made of the oldest inhabitants about who had drilled the hole, and the answer was always the same—the hole in the boulder was there when the first settlers came. Thus we have the testimony of a member of the very first group of settlers to take land in Polk County and several neighboring counties who were the first white men known to have seen Cormorant Lake. It was written in 1945 by Mr. E. O. Estenson, a highly respected citizen of Crookston, Minnesota:

> In the spring of 1870, my father and some other men set out from Hartland near Albert Lea, Minnesota, to look for land in the northern part of the State. I was permitted to go along. I was then ten and a half years old. We had a team of horses and a covered wagon.
>
> After traveling several hundred miles, we came to Cormorant Lake in Becker County. We were now well beyond the last settlers. The entire Red River Valley and the

surrounding parts were empty of white men, excepting for a few Indian forts and Hudson Bay trading posts. We camped on the west side of this lake, near its northern end. Here we caught some fish. We had no boat, but there were some big rocks there, and the water was deep enough so we could fish from the shore. We cleaned our fish on these rocks and noticed a neatly drilled hole in one of them. We were puzzled to find this drilled hole, but thought that the Indians had somehow made it. We then turned northwest and followed the Red River for about sixty miles until we came to a spot, later known as Frog Point, about five miles northwest of Climax in Polk County. Here we found very good land and settled, but we first continued north into Canada.

On our return to Hartland we stopped again and fished at Cormorant Lake. It was very easy to locate the rocks because a small naked rocky island lay a few hundred feet off shore. While my father was cleaning the fish, I was poking in the crevice between two big rocks and found a small firesteel. The next year, 1871, we moved up and became permanent settlers, the first white settlers in Polk County.

E. O. Estenson[7]

Some readers may question the need of ringbolts or iron pins for securing the boat. Why not camp on a river where the painter could be tied to a tree on the bank?

The answer is that this was a most important measure for safety. A camp on a river or stream could be surrounded by an enemy and every camper would be killed. A camp on the shore of a lake would leave at least one direction of escape. But that depended on the possibility of a quick departure. It would not do to pull the boat high up on the beach because it would take some time to get it afloat. The ringbolt in a hole of a boulder was far more safe. A rush could be made for the boat, the last man aboard would flip out the ringbolt, and the boat would be afloat.

Wahlgren thinks that they may be surveyor's marks or were drilled for the purpose of removing obstructions in farming operations. It is true that a government surveyor sometimes has need of a hole in a rock and an iron pin to mark a section corner, but none of the ten holes here mentioned were found on section or quarter corners. It is also true that farmers sometimes drilled holes in rocks that interfered with plowing. But this has nothing to do with stones on the beach which are not obstructing farm operations. Mr. Wahlgren has difficulty in understanding the function and location of mooring stones. He says:

> Local reconnoitering has resulted in the conclusion that the majority of these [holes] have been drilled by farmers in preparation for abandoned attempts at black powder blasting. Several such holes—not mentioned by Holand—are plainly visible on the Flaten and Ohman properties today.[8]

This shows a lack of comprehension of the significance of a mooring stone. The only place where a mooring stone belongs or can be found is at the highest level of a lake or former lake. Stones with chiseled holes found in cultivated fields have nothing to do with mooring stones.

As these travelers came from a salt sea in the north, they must have come from Hudson Bay. No attempt has been made to look for mooring stones along the Nelson River.

On arriving in Lake Winnipeg, explorers found a different situation. This lake is about three hundred miles long and the travelers must have spent a half dozen days and nights on its shore. As the lake is flanked by a rocky beach, this would necessitate mooring holes in the rocky bank of sheltered harbors. Some years ago I went up to Berens River on Lake Winnipeg with several companions. The estuary of this river is a bay many miles long, and there are at least a hundred islands, mostly very small. Being unable to get a small boat immediately, we spent two or three days in following the shore, and then the steamer came on its return voyage and we were obliged to leave.

Before leaving Berens River, I made the acquaintance of a Norwegian fisherman named Evald Hansen, who lived on one of the larger islands. I explained to him the purpose of my visit and asked him to look around for a mooring stone, which he promised to do.

Many years went by, when I finally had a letter from him. He had found a mooring hole on an island covering about two acres, lying about one and a half miles from the Berens River post office. The mooring hole is about seven inches deep and its axis toward the water as is shown by the photograph where Mr. Hansen's youngest son is standing close to the mooring hole (see Figure 13). The reader will note that the axis of this mooring hole leans more toward the water than do the holes in Minnesota. This is because the hole is much higher in position than these, and a greater inclination was necessary to make it possible to flip the ringbolt loose from the boat.

Mr. Hansen in his letter makes the following important remarks about the Lake Winnipeg water level:

> Getting back to the mooring stone, I went to the Island, lot 16, and measured the water level May 22 (1957). The water level is now 20 feet below the hole. The water has dropped something terrible since last fall. Its been a very dry year not much snow last winter and no rain at all this spring. . . . We had very high water level here for the last 10 years, so I guess its on the drop again.

Mr. Hansen wrote that he had heard there was a mooring stone near Warren's landing. He also said that Leaf River Point was formerly called *White Men's Writing on the Rock*. This inlet is about thirty miles northwest of Berens River.

Because of lack of money for traveling expenses, no further search for mooring stones on the shore of Lake Winnipeg has been made.

The following is a report on the route followed by the explorers through Minnesota as shown by the mooring stones (see Figure X showing exact route). The inscription says that these men came from the north, and as Red River is the only waterway that leads south, they must have followed this river. On reaching Buffalo River, which joins the Red a few miles north of Fargo, they ascended the Buffalo because their intention, presumably, was to return to their headquarters in Vinland, far to the southeast, and the channel of the Buffalo leads southeast.

After ascending this river for two days, the explorers found that the river channel made a turn of ninety degrees and continued in a northeasterly direction. But toward the southeast they saw a string of lakes (probably one big lake at that time), extending as far southeast as they could see. This must have seemed promising, but on proceeding six or seven miles, they came to the end of the lake or lakes. Here, on the south side of the lake, they made camp because here they left mooring stone No. 1.

This mooring stone lies just behind the buildings of the late O. N. Bjorndal in section 12, Skree township, about seven miles straight south from the village of Hawley. Mr. Bjorndal was not among the early settlers who came in the 1870's, but being an intelligent man, he inquired of them if they knew anything about this big stone with a deep hole in it. He found it was well known, because stones are rare on the Red River bottom, and many men had noted the hole in the stone. No one knew who had drilled the hole because this was done before the first settlers came.

There is no lake now where the stone lies, but on inquiry it was learned that there formerly had been a lake there which was drained by help of a big county ditch in 1906. This lake was rich in fish.[9]

As the explorers now found themselves in a dead end, without any lake or watercourse leading east or south, the only thing they could do was to return to the river and follow it upstream, in the hope of finding a way around the high land to the east. They did so, and about ten miles up the river they came to a small lake. Here, on the south side of this former lake, they left mooring stone No. 2. The distance from stone No. 1 to No. 2 is about sixteen miles which would take a whole day as part of the distance was against the current of the river.

Information about this second mooring stone came to me through Mr. Bjorndal who wrote me that a mooring stone was found near Hawley. In order to verify this, I wrote to Rev. S. G.

Figure 1. The Kensington Stone

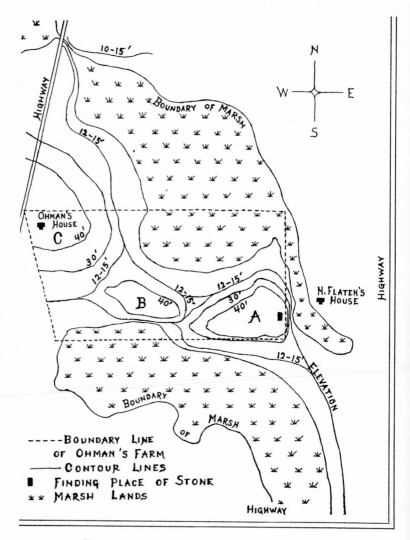

Legend on map:

N
W — E
S

10-15'
Boundary of Marsh
12-15
Highway
Ohman's House
C 40'
30'
12-15'
B 40'
12-5'
12-15'
30'
40'
A
N. Flaten's House
Highway
12-15' Elevation
Boundary
of
Marsh
Highway

----- Boundary Line of Ohman's Farm
——— Contour Lines
▮ Finding Place of Stone
⚹⚹ Marsh Lands

FIGURE 2.   Contour Sketch of Finding Place

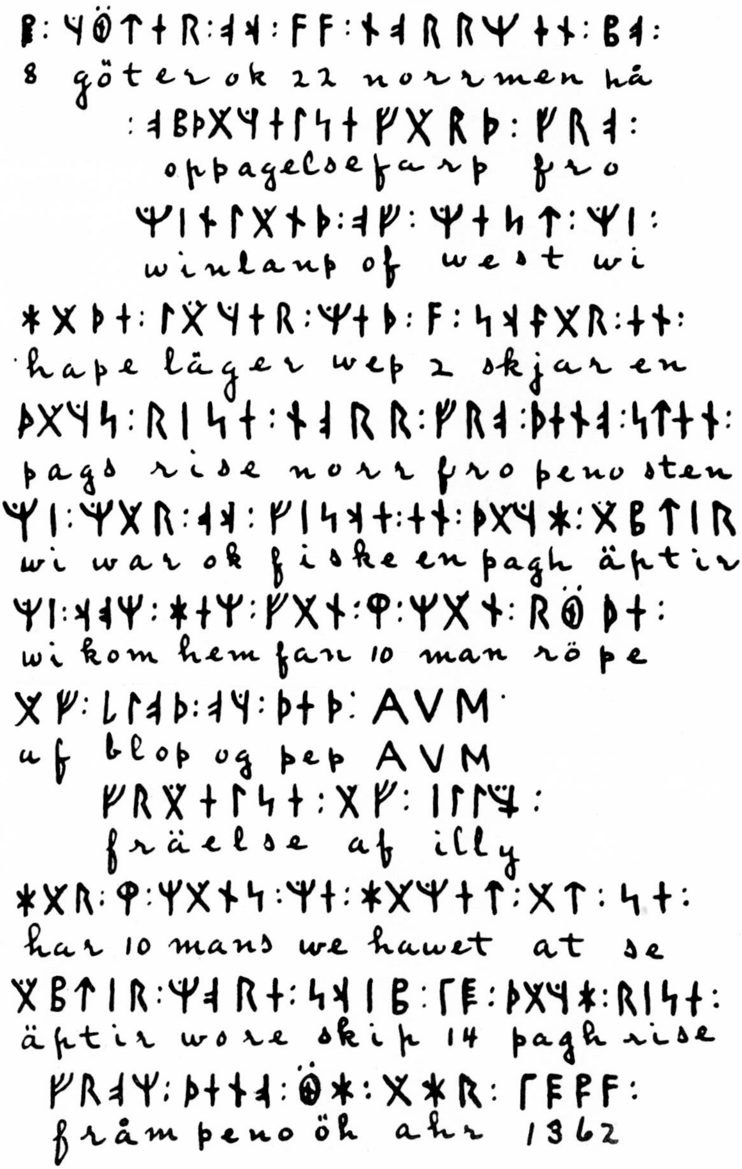

ᛒ: ᚴᚯᛏᛆᚱ:ᛰᛰ: FF:ᛰᛰ ᚱᚱᚤ ᛏᛏ: ᛒᛰ:
8 göter ok 22 norrmen hå

: ᛰᛒᛈᚴᚤᛏᚠᛰᛏ ᚠᚷᚱᚦ: ᚠᚱᛰ:
oppagelsefarþ fro

ᚤᛰᛏᚠᚷᛰᚦ:ᛰᚠ: ᚤᛏᚼᛏ:ᚤᛰ:
winlanþ of west wi

ᚼᚷᚦᛏ: ᚠᚷᚤᛏᚱ:ᚤᛏᚦ: F:ᚼᛰᚠᚷᚱ:ᛏᛏ:
hape läger wep 2 skjar en

ᚦᚷᚤᛋ:ᚱᛁᚼᛏ:ᛰᛰ ᚱᚱ:ᚠᚱᛰ ᚦᛏᛰᛰ ᚼᛏᛏᛏ:
pags ride norr fro peno sten

ᚤᛰ:ᚤᚷᚱ:ᛰᛰ: ᚠᛁᚼᛰᛏ:ᛏᛏ ᚦᚷᚤ✳:ᚷᛒᛏᛁᚱ
wi war ok fiske en pagh äptir

ᚤᛁ:ᚼᛰᚤ:✳ᛏᚤ:ᚠᚷᛏ:ᛦ:ᚤᚷᛏ: ᚱᚯ ᚦᛏ:
wi kom hem fan 10 man röpe

ᚷᚠ:�└᛬ᚱᛰᚦ:ᛰᚤ:ᚦᛏᚦ: AVM·
uf blop og þeþ AVM

ᚠᚱᚷᛏᚠᚼᛏ:ᚷᚠ: ᛁᚠᚠᚤ:
fräelse af illy

✳ᚷᚱ:ᛦ:ᚤᚷᛏᚼ:ᚤᛏ:✳ᚷᚤᛏᛏ:ᚷᛏ:ᚼᛏ:
har 10 mans we hawet at se

ᚤᛒᛏᛁᚱ:ᚤᛰᚱᛏ:ᚼᚼᛁᛒ:ᚠᛖ:ᚦᚷᚤ✳:ᚱᛁᚼᛏ:
äptir wore skip 14 pagh rise

ᚠᚱᛰᚤ:ᚦᛏᛏᛰ:ᚯ✳:ᚷ✳ᚱ: ᚠᛖᚠF:
främ þeno öh ahr 1362

FIGURE 3. Transliteration of the Kensington Inscription

131

Figure 4. Olof Ohman

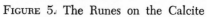

Figure 5. The Runes on the Calcite

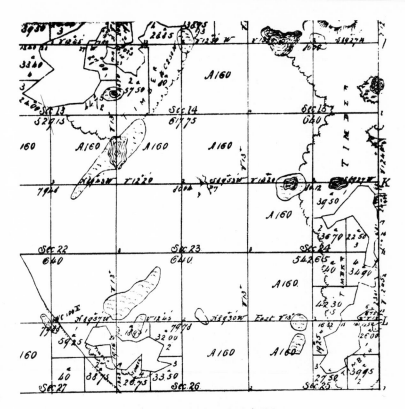

FIGURE 6. Old Surveyor's Map

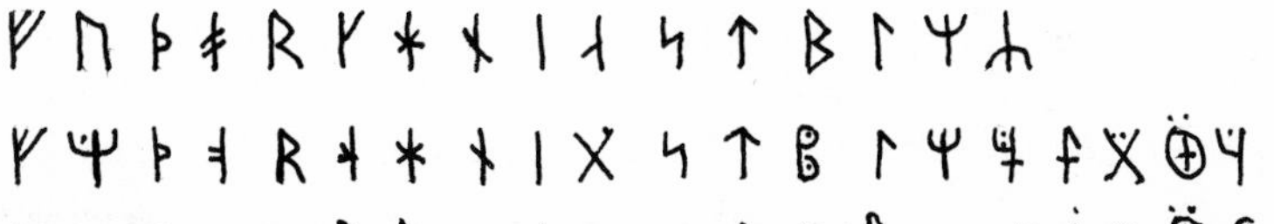

ᚠᚢᚦᚨᚱᚲᚷᚺᚾᛁᛁᛇᛈᛒᛚᛗᛜ
ᚠᚢᚦᚨᚱᚲᚷᚺᚾᛁᛇᛈᛒᛚᛗᛜᛟᛞᚷ

𝓯 𝓾 𝓭 𝓸 𝓻 𝓴 𝓴 𝓷 𝓲 𝓪 𝓼 𝓽 𝓹 𝓵 𝓶 𝔂 𝓳 𝓪 Ö 𝓰

FIGURE 7. Rosander's Runes and the Kensington Stone

THE RUNIC SYMBOLS

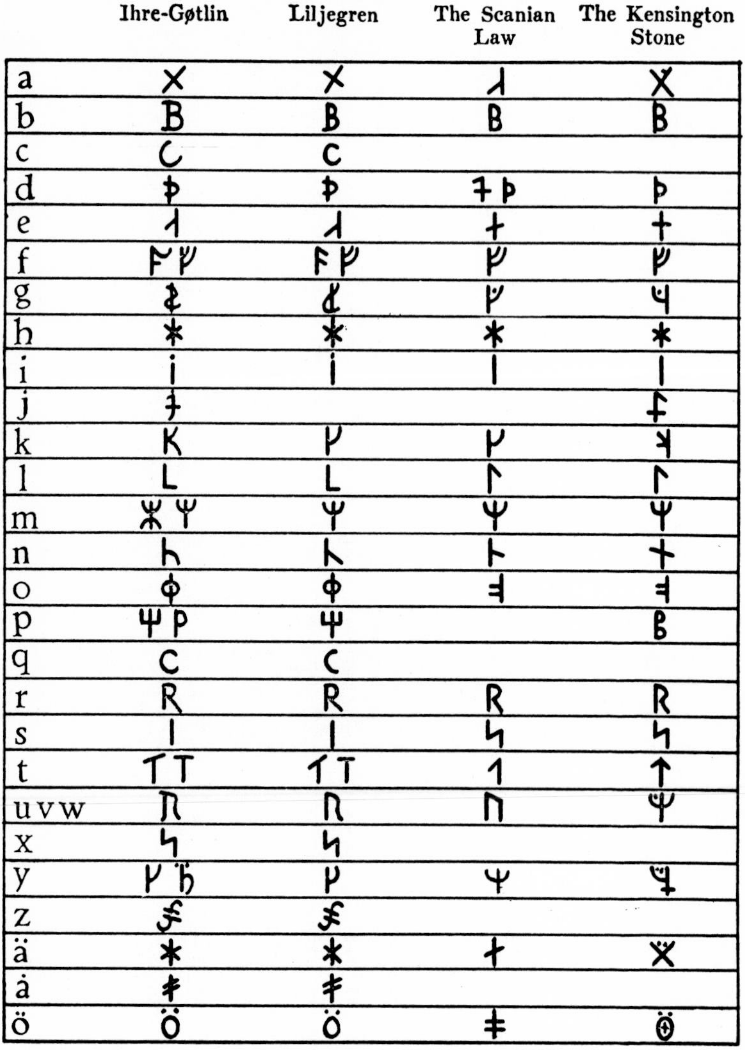

	Ihre-Gøtlin	Liljegren	The Scanian Law	The Kensington Stone
a	✕	✕	⟨⟩	✕
b	B	B	B	B
c	C	C		
d	Þ	Þ	⊤ Þ	Þ
e	⟨	⟨	+	+
f	⟨⟩ ⟨⟩	⟨⟩ ⟨⟩	⟨⟩	⟨⟩
g	⟨	⟨	⟨⟩	⟨⟩
h	✳	✳	✳	✳
i	⟨	⟨	⟨	⟨
j	⟨			⟨
k	K	⟨⟩	⟨⟩	⟨
l	L	L	⟨	⟨
m	⟨⟩ ⟨⟩	⟨⟩	⟨⟩	⟨⟩
n	⟨	⟨	⟨	⟨
o	⟨⟩	⟨⟩	⟨	⟨
p	⟨⟩ ⟨⟩	⟨⟩		B
q	C	C		
r	R	R	R	R
s	⟨	⟨	⟨	⟨
t	⟨ T	⟨ T	⟨	⟨
u v w	⟨	⟨	⟨	⟨⟩
x	⟨	⟨		
y	⟨⟩ ⟨⟩	⟨⟩	⟨⟩	⟨⟩
z	⟨	⟨		
ä	✳	✳	+	✕
å	⟨	⟨		
ö	Ö	Ö	⟨	⟨

FIGURE 8. Four Runic Alphabets of the Middle Ages

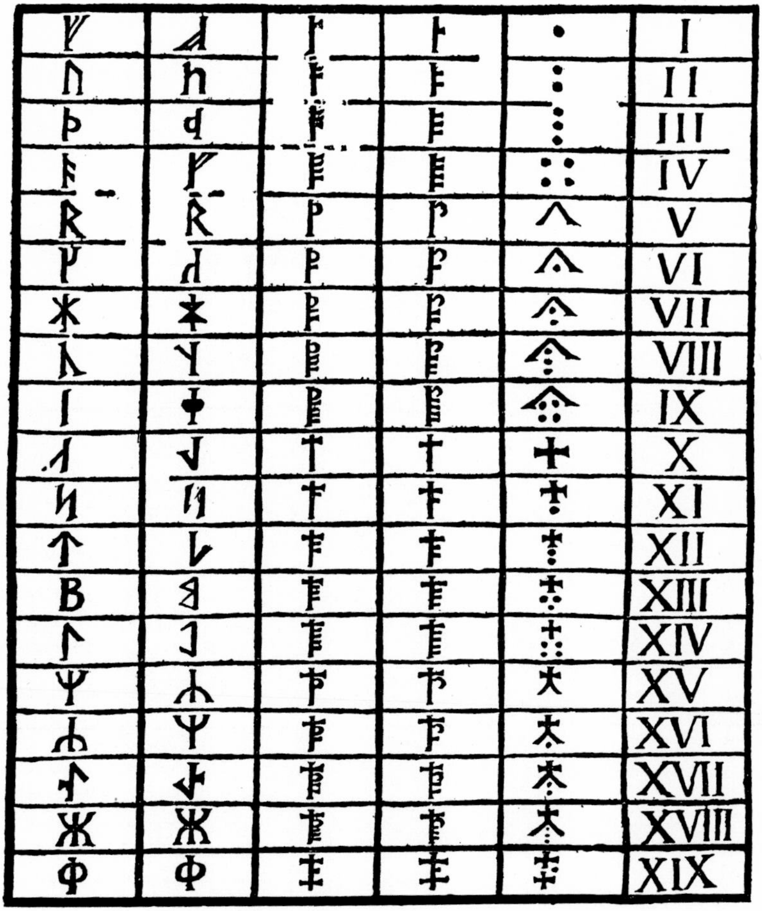

FIGURE 9. Runic Numerals of 1328

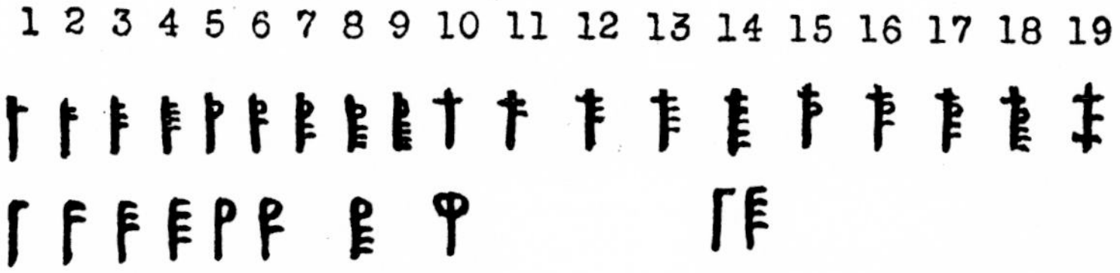

1 2 3 4 5 6 7 8 9 10 11 12 13 14 15 16 17 18 19

FIGURE 10. Runic Numerals on the Kensington Stone

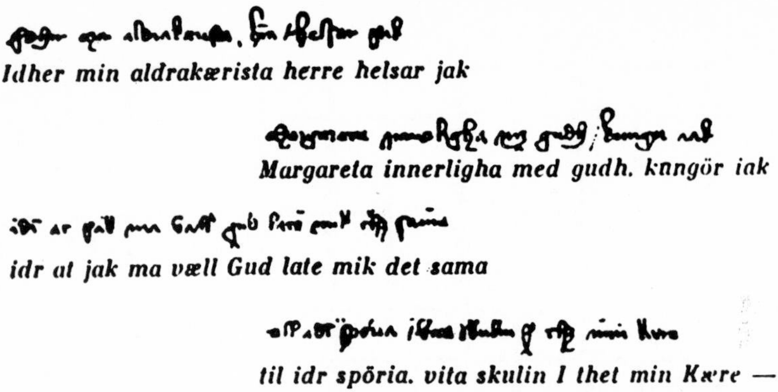

Idher min aldrakærista herre helsar jak

Margareta innerligha med gudh. knngör iak

idr at jak ma væll Gud late mik det sama

til idr spöria. vita skulin I thet min Kære —

FIGURE 11. First Lines of Queen Margaret's Letter

FIGURE 12. Hedberg's Copy of the Inscription

FIGURE 13.
Mooring Stone on
Lake Winnipeg

FIGURE 14. Ruysch Map of Arctic Regions

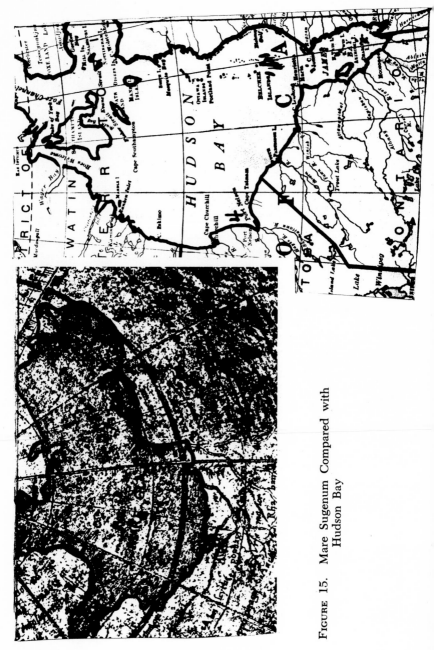

FIGURE 15. Mare Sugenum Compared with
Hudson Bay

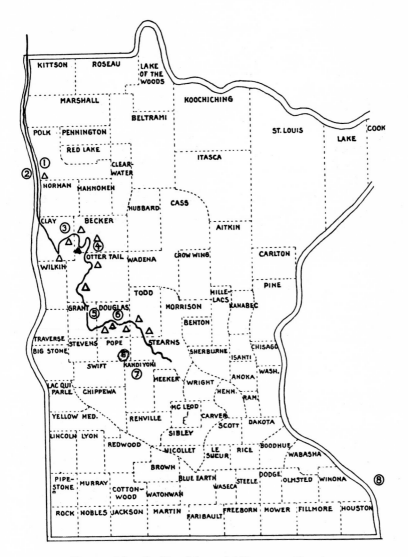

FIGURE 16.   Outline Map of Minnesota Showing
Concentration of Mooring Stones

FIGURE 17. The Big Stone Near Sauk Centre

FIGURE 18. Reconstruction of Altar at Sauk Lake

The Cormorant Fire-steel

The Detroit Lakes Fire-steel

The Climax Fire-steel

FIGURE 19.   Three Firesteels

FIGURE 20. The Knox Halberd

FIGURE 21. The Estenson
Halberd

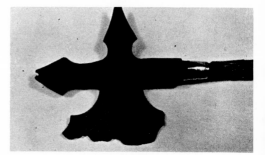

FIGURE 22. A Ceremonial Halberd Becomes a Modern
Tobacco Cutter

FIGURE 23. The Republic Axe

FIGURE 24.	FIGURE 25.	FIGURE 26.
The Erdahl Axe	The Mora Axe	The Norway Lake
		Battle Axe

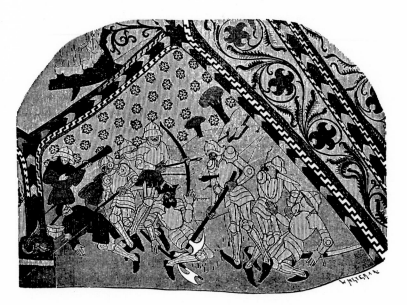

FIGURE 27.   Painting Showing the Axe

143

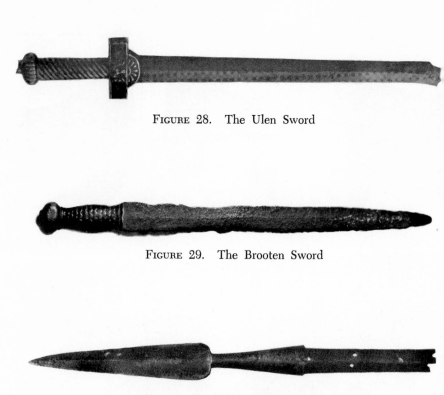

FIGURE 28.   The Ulen Sword

FIGURE 29.   The Brooten Sword

FIGURE 30.   The Windjue Spear

FIGURE 31.   The Boat Hook

Hauge who for forty years had served as pastor of a group of congregations in and near Hawley. The following is his reply.

HAWLEY, MINN. Nov. 13, 1939

I never heard of this stone until I got your letter. Guided by Mr. Bjorndal, I drove out to its finding place, two miles east of Hawley. . . . The stone lies on a slope on the east side of a narrow coulee which has a smooth, even bottom. This coulee may have been a bay of a former lake because it comes to an abrupt end at its head toward the south. This region is a wilderness of high stoney hills, inhabited only by wolves, and no settler would think of clearing land here . . .

The stone is very large and the hole which is eight inches deep and triangular is weathered so smooth as to seem like glass on the inside. Bjorndal, who had measurements with him, found that in its diameter and position it was just the same as the hole in his own stone and in the stone at Cormorant Lake. It is now about twenty feet above the water level. It is not difficult to understand that the water may have been that high as it has been almost that high since I came here forty years ago. It is a most remarkable discovery, for it is plain to everyone that the hole was not bored or drilled since white men settled in this region.

S. G. HAUGE

It is likely that the main group of these early travelers had a couple of scouts whose duty each day was to choose the most promising course for the next day's travel. These scouts could report that just above this lake the river divided in two. The main stream came from the northeast, but a smaller branch came from a lake about four miles up the east branch. Beyond that point the course seemed promising, but the four miles to the lake were up a small stream with many obstructions.

The travelers decided to take this easterly branch, but it must have taken them all day because it was necessary to drag the boat almost all the way. Finally they came to campsite No. 3 at the west end of Stinking Lake in Becker County. It was the shortest distance covered in one day, but probably the most laborious on the entire trip. Mooring stone No. 3 now lies in the muck bottom of the lake, close to the shore and near the outlet. Here the bank is very steep, and it is probable that the mooring stone at one time was a part of the bank, and then through erosion slid down into the lake.

The distance from stone No. 3 to No. 4 is only about ten miles through a string of small lakes. But just before reaching campsite No. 4 they came to a ridge about forty feet high and almost a quarter mile wide. A portage was necessary here which would take about a half day, and then they came to Nelson Lake at the south end of the portage. This was a small but deep lake with good fishing.

Nelson Lake connects with West Cormorant Lake to the south, a shallow bottom, which in turn connects with Big Cormorant to the east where we find mooring stone No. 5.

The first man known to have seen the mooring stone at Cormorant Lake was E. O. Estenson, as mentioned above.

Another early visitor was Ole Larson in Barnesville, Minnesota. I have a letter from him telling of his first visit to Cormorant Lake in 1879. He was then twelve years old. He says the hole in the stone was then about four feet above the lake level. "At that time, 1879, no one lived around the lake, but there were many Indian tents and campfires seen."[10]

The distance traveled from campsite 4 to 5 is eighteen miles.

Cormorant Lake has one of the highest elevations in the state, its normal stage being 1,353 feet above the sea level. It has no confluents, being fed only by the rainfall. For this reason it will eventually be merely a marsh. At present it is too low to have an outlet, but when Estenson saw it in 1870, a brook issued from it on the south side. This meandered down through a swamp and joined Pelican Lake, sixty feet lower in altitude. This lake is fed by Pelican River and is one of the few lakes which has maintained its ancient level by means of a dike. In a little harbor near this outlet is mooring stone No. 6. From stone 5 to 6 is about eighteen miles of easy voyaging.

The explorers now entered Pelican River, a stream formerly of considerable size, down which they floated southward for about fifty miles. It is not likely that they camped on the way as they could easily make five miles an hour without touching an oar, and they did not need to stop for hunting as plenty of fish could be caught from the yawl.

But about six miles southwest of the present city of Fergus Falls the river makes an abrupt turn to the west. From a neighboring elevation the travelers could easily see its course, marked by a belt of timber, running as far westward as the eye could follow it. At this turn of the river they probably made their camp. As they needed no mooring stone here, this camp-site is not marked.

As the terrain to the south of this place is very rough and hilly, they would not go that way. To the east lies a fairly level area with many small lakes. This appears to be the course they took because this leads to Pomme de Terre River which flows through Ten Mile Lake, where we find the next mooring stone.

This stone lies on the northeast side of the lower lake, perhaps a mile from the isthmus that divides the lake. Originally it must have been a part of a very steep bank which shows marks of much erosion. The distance from the big bend in the river mentioned above, where the explorers must have camped, to mooring stone No. 7 is about twenty miles. This may have taken two days.

They were now again on a river flowing southward, and this they followed for about twenty-five miles. But this tendency of all rivers to run southward or westward must have been annoying to them because they wanted to go east, to Vinland. We therefore see them at Lake Barrett, where they appear to have camped, turning away from the gently flowing Pomme de Terre River to take an eastward course through a succession of swamps and lakes. About twelve miles east of Lake Barrett they came to a lake called Venus, and here we find another mooring stone, the eighth. This lake lies in the *center* of Urness township. At this center point there is a private road running east to the lake, about seven hundred feet. Here the mooring stone lies about seventy-five feet west of a rickety bridge over a very narrow passage of water which connects the southern part of Lake Venus with the northern. The hole for the ringbolt is only 4½ inches deep, which was probably considered sufficient as the anchorage was in a sheltered spot. From here a waterway runs east and south to the former lake on Ohman's farm, a distance of about twelve miles.

On arriving at Ohman's lake, the travelers finally came to a region where the drainage was eastward, and here, across the southern part of Douglas County, we find a succession of mooring stones. The first of these (the tenth of all) is on the shore of Lake Latoka, about three miles southwest of Alexandria. I did not hear of this until the summer of 1960, and although I have been there twice since it was found, I have not yet learned enough about it to give a proper report on the circumstances of its discovery.

The eleventh mooring stone is found on the beach of Lake Jessie, about five miles southeast of Alexandria, but by boat it is about fifteen miles from the mooring stone on the shore of Lake Latoka. Lake Jessie can never have been any higher than it is now because it is at the head of a long string of lakes.[11]

The southeastern part of Douglas County is flat, treeless, and poorly drained. There is an old watercourse east of Lake Jessie which leads to Lake Osakis, but even without this there would be little difficulty for ten men and a boat to follow the grassy swales down to Lake Osakis.

Some years ago my son Harold and I searched the shore of the village of Osakis for a mooring stone. A couple of miles east he found several big boulders, one of which appeared to have been intended for a mooring stone. He found in the top of it a chiselled hole about an inch deep. It did not seem likely that this hole was made by a pioneer farmer in search of building stone as it lay on the beach at the foot of a perpendicular cut in the bank about twelve feet high. More likely it was an abortive effort, and we thought that the mooring hole may have been in one of the other big rocks which may have been overturned by the shoving of the ice early in spring. As we could do nothing more at that time, further investigation was postponed.

Many years later, Mr. Holiday Phillips made a trip up into Minnesota to inspect the mooring stones which he had read about in one of my books. During his travels he came to Lake Osakis and found the hole described above. Believing that the true mooring stone was one of the other big boulders, he went down to the village and hired the necessary equipment and men to move and turn over one or more of the other boulders.

In the middle of this job a man named Roy T. Davis drove by and stopped to ask what was going on. He was told that they were looking for a stone with a one-inch hole in it, quite deep.

"A stone with a hole in it? Why that's up to my place, about a half-mile along the beach."

"Is it there now?"

"Sure it's there, but it's covered up with four feet of concrete. I saw it nine years ago when I moved up here. Of course, I did not then know what it was, but I remember the hole, about six inches deep. The next year I decided to build a good boathouse, and so we slid the big stone down a few feet and leveled off the base for a boathouse, so that no shoving of the ice could move it."

"How much will it cost to uncover it?"

"Oh, I'd say about a hundred dollars to tear it apart and another hundred to repair it."

However, it was found that it was not necessary to tear the foundation apart to prove that mooring stone was there. Carl Anderson, a highly respected farmer near by, said he had seen the mooring stone many times before Davis built his boathouse.

The outlet of Lake Osakis is the Sauk River which leads southeast to the Mississippi at St. Cloud. Nothing is known about how far these ancient travelers floated down this river or what later happened to them. As shown above, the explorers spent about thirteen days in traveling from Buffalo River to the outlet of Lake Osakis. Twelve of those campsites are marked with mooring stones. In addition we have a campsite near Climax in Polk County, Minn., which will be described in a following chapter and a true mooring stone on an island in the harbor of Berens Rivers, Manitoba, which makes a total distance of about six hundred miles, not including the Nelson or Hayes Rivers.

A memento of another kind, but apparently of the same travelers, may be seen about five miles northeast of Sauk Centre. This is described in the next chapter.

chapter fourteen

THE ALTAR IN THE WILDERNESS

In the fall of 1943, Rev. Henry Retzek, rector of St. Alexius Church, West Union, Minn., wrote to me about a very large rock which had what appeared to be four mooring holes on its upper surface (see Figure 17). His informant was Mr. Frank L. Gettys, Great Northern station agent at Sauk Centre, whose father had owned the farm on which the rock was found and was the first to clear land on it. Father Retzek sent me six photographs which he had taken of the rock. As this rock apparently has a very special significance, it will be described here as fully as possible.

Upon writing to Mr. Gettys, the son, for a personal statement, I received the following reply:

SAUK CENTRE, MINN., NOV. 29, 1943.

As I recollect, my father bought the farm in 1890 or 1892. It lies about five miles northeast of Sauk Centre in Section 26 of Birchdale Township in Todd County. I believe my father paid $3.50 an acre for the land. It had been logged recently and was covered with brush and big stumps. No one had lived on it before that time, and he was the first to clear land there.

My earliest recollection of this farm and stone came about in going out to it to help my father pick potatoes that he had broken up soil for in spring. Believe it was in the fall of 1892. The reason it stands out so vivid in my mind was, we walked the entire distance out and back besides doing a hard days work. I was so tired when we reached home I could not sleep that night. This patch of ground did not cover over an acre and was all there was cleared at that time. The balance of the farm was covered with large stumps. It took us many years with oxen to clear the land and prepare it for a farm.

We boys played around the BIG ROCK as it was known then. What excited our curiosity most was the holes in the side and bottom. At that time I was about 11 years old. I was born in 1882. I have just talked with a man who is 74 years old who cut cordwood on my father's farm many years before he bought it. He says he saw the four holes in the big rock when he was a little boy. It is located 1½ mile east of Sauk Lake on the edge of an old river bed which can be plainly seen.

FRANK L. GETTYS

In the latter part of April, 1944, I examined the rock, accompanied by Rev. Mr. Retzek, Rev. Mr. Kramer, D.C.L., of Sauk Centre, and my son Harold Holand, of Milwaukee. We found that the rock was lying on the lower slope of what may have been an inlet of Sauk Lake, but scarcely a river bed because there were no gullied banks. The rock is a huge boulder twenty-seven feet long by seventeen feet wide. It is practically semi-circular in its horizontal outline. The upper surface is concave, with a uniform slope toward the straight side. As shown in the photograph, it has some resemblance to the choir of a small church or a miniature amphitheater (see Figure 17).

Four holes have been drilled into the stone in different directions. The two holes to which the man in the picture is pointing have a horizontal axis and are twelve inches apart. The rock at this place has a vertical surface. Fifteen and a half feet from these holes, on the hither side of the concave depression, is seen a curving white line made by a slender limb which marks the spot of the third hole. This hole is almost vertical. Another twig is seen twenty-nine inches nearer the camera, marking the spot of the fourth hole, the axis of which is oblique. This is nineteen inches inside the near edge of the stone.

The depths and diameters of these holes are not the same. The two horizontal holes are six and nine inches deep, and their diameter is about one and three-eighths inches. The third hole is sixteen inches deep and one inch in diameter.

Upon inquiry, it was learned that the man who had the

earliest recollection of the rock was Everton B. Harder, of Eagle
Bend, Minnesota. A letter was sent to him, asking him to tell
what he knew about the rock. The following is his reply:

EAGLE BEND, MINN., April 30, 1944.

In reply to your inquiry about the big rock near Sauk
Lake I will say that we moved into that neighborhood
March 3, 1883 when I was 13 years old. The land was
rough, hilly and stony and covered with timber. When we
came there were only four settlers around there and they
were several miles apart. My first experience in regard to
this rock came the same spring when hunting cattle on
horseback. I was following a small trail through the timber
when the horse saw the rock and made such a sudden turn
that I was left sitting in the mud. Hundreds of times I
have stood on that rock and listened for the cow bell as
there was no herd law then—all cattle ran at large. I often
whiled away my time by poking in the holes of the rock
with a wire. The rock then was all in one piece with some
checks or fissues. Now I hear that there is a big crack in it.

In the winter of 1886 and 87 I cut cordwood around that
rock as well as on other parts of the land. We were cutting
for a man named W. S. Dean, an implement dealer in
Sauk Centre, and M. E. Dimon who lived two miles northeast of the rock. The first owner of the land was a man
named Spriesterfauch who lived about ten miles southwest
of Sauk Centre.

There was fine spring a few rods below the rock; but as
the timber was cut it finally dried up. I am now in my
75th year.

EVERTON B. HARDER

Mr. Harder later sent me a map showing every quarter
section in an area of twelve square miles around the rock. In
this he shows the location of the five first settlers, including his
father, whose farm was nearest to the rock.

Inasmuch as the holes were seen about ten years before
anyone made any clearing on the land, the theory that the holes
were drilled for the purpose of making the land fit for cultiva-

tion is pretty well excluded. Another conceivable purpose is that the holes were drilled for the purpose of obtaining building stone. But this theory seems to be equally untenable. All the surrounding area abounds in surface boulders. On the forty-acre tract where the stone lies, more than five hundred wagonloads of stone have been picked up and thrown in piles, and much of the land is still too stony for cultivation. The early farmers made no use of stone in building, as they found logs more serviceable for both houses and barns. Sauk Centre, five miles away, in 1883 was a small pioneer village with a few scattered houses, none of which were built of stone. If any of these pioneers needed stone for a cellar, it is hardly plausible that he would have gone five miles back into the woods and there made an unsuccessful attack upon a huge boulder when there were plenty of stones in his own backyard.

The stone at present is split in two, leaving a crevice from eight to twelve inches wide and about fifteen feet long. This crevice makes a turn of 90° immediately to one side of one of the drilled holes. Mr. Gettys and Mr. Harder say this is of recent origin. This was also the opinion of the late Father Retzek, who was a geologist of some note.[1]

It is not likely that any of the holes in this big rock served as a mooring place for the boat of the explorers. Neither of the two horizontal holes could have been made for this purpose, because the tugging of the boat would have pulled out the ringbolt. Furthermore, there would be no need for a mooring stone at this place, even if the cove extended up to the big rock. At the head of a long and narrow inlet there would be no wave action, the trees would be growing close to the water, and the boat could be tied to a tree. We must therefore seek another explanation for the purpose of these holes.

Since the time when their existence was made known, in the fall of 1943, these holes have been inspected by many. It is the consensus of local opinion that the two horizontal holes, twelve inches apart, can have been made only for the reception of two brackets which carried a small shelf or table. This is a logical conclusion. But what was the purpose of this table? As the holes wherein the brackets were fixed are only twelve inches apart, the table top would necessarily be very small. Here was a real puzzle.

Finally a suggestion was made which opened a most interesting perspective. It was recalled that the Kensington inscription indicates that a priest was a member of the expedition—just as we find one or more priests as members of every French exploration party in America in the seventeenth century. This priest had certain duties to perform for the spiritual welfare of his companions. One of these duties was the celebration of the Holy Mass. In order to celebrate the Mass, an altar was necessary, and the shelf or table was perhaps constructed to serve this purpose.[2] The Church recognized the need of portable altars for use by missionaries among savages, and by members of expeditions in the wilderness, and regulated their form, substance, and service.

> A portable altar consists of a small natural stone which must be sufficiently hard to resist every fracture. It must be consecrated by a bishop. . . . It is inserted in or placed upon the table of the altar, about two inches from the front edge, and in such a manner that, by its slight elevation above the table, the celebrant can trace its outline with his hand and thus recognize its location beneath the altar cloth. In general it should be large enough to hold the Sacred Host and the greater part of the base of the chalice. . . . Five Greek crosses (representing the five wounds of Jesus on the cross) are engraved on it, one near each corner and one in the centre to indicate the places on which the unctions are made at the consecration. . . . The table and supports on which the portable altar rests may be constructed of any suitable material, wood or stone, covered with an altar cloth of silk or linen.[3]

We see, then, that a portable altar was not a ready-made table, which would have been an awkward burden to carry around, but, essentially, a small flat stone consecrated by a bishop for a special use. But a table on which to place this stone was necessary, and here is where the shelf on the big rock fits in. As the priest is standing, while officiating at the altar, it is desirable that the altar table be of the most convenient height, which is at the waist line, and altars in all Catholic churches are therefore of this uniform height—from forty to forty-two inches. Upon removing the loose stones that had been thrown in on the sloping floor of the rock, it was found that the altar stone would be about forty inches above the spot where the priest would have stood.

The presence of this table on which to place the altar stone also explains why the two horizontal holes have a bigger diameter than the other holes. It would have been an inexcusable carelessness if the brackets underneath the altar table broke, and the sacred vessels and consecrated bread and wine fell down. To guard against such a mishap, the two horizontal holes were made extra large, so that strong brackets could be used.

The placement of the altar at this particular part of the rock shows reverent precaution and forethought. The vertical side of the stone here rises to a height of seven feet above its stone floor, and gives the best possible protection against a sudden gust of wind which might lift the consecrated host off the altar. Then, too, Catholic altars are preferably placed against an opaque background so that nothing will disturb the devout attention of the worshippers while Mass is celebrated. At this spot the vertical background was present, and here an altar crucifix may have been placed.

The identification of the two horizontal holes at the first necessary step in making an altar also explains the significance of the other two holes. The service at the altar was regulated by a time-honored ritual. One requirement was that the altar table should be illuminated by candles when Mass was celebrated.[4] Furthermore, "these candles should be lighted before Mass begins and remain lighted until it is finished,"[5] and *nothing*, be it attack by enemies or disturbance of nature, must be permitted to interrupt the celebration of the Mass. As this altar was in the open air, it was necessary to take precautions lest the candles be extinguished by a sudden gust of wind. The best way to prevent this would be to construct a canopy over the altar. Such canopies are also prescribed in the ritual, and are thus described in the *Catholic Encyclopaedia:* "A canopy should

be suspended over the altar. It should be square in form, sufficiently large to cover the altar and the predella on which the
celebrant stands. . . . It is either suspended from the ceiling by
a movable chain . . . or it may be attached to the wall."[6]

It was not difficult to put a canopy over the altar in the
big rock, because the right "wing" and the rear edge of the
stone have approximately the same elevation, and are sufficiently
high to make unnecessary any supports on these two sides. The
sail of the boat could be spread over these two sides and kept in
position by a few rocks. It remained to put up a support for
the canopy at the fourth corner, and this could be done by
drilling a vertical hole at the desired spot. This hole would
necessarily have to be quite deep, lest a sudden gust of wind
lift the canopy and dislodge the support. Here we have an
adequate explanation why hole number three (where the support was placed) is so much deeper, sixteen inches, than the
others. This hole is just big enough to receive the shaft of a
spear of the kind carried by the explorers.[7] If a long-handled
halberd were lashed to the upper part of the spear, this would
provide a neat support of the right height. In order to prevent
the sail-canopy from sagging in the middle, an inclined guy
line would have to be stretched from the top of the support at
the fourth corner. This need explains the presence of the fourth
hole, twenty-nine inches to the left of the support (hole number
three), which is in the right spot for anchoring such a guy line.
Finally, we have the requirement that the canopy be square, as
stated above. As the length and width of this canopy would be
about sixteen feet each way, this requirement was also complied
with. When completed, the rock altar and canopy would appear
much like the accompanying sketch. (See Figure 18.)

These explorers and their priest no doubt celebrated the
Mass at frequent intervals, so it is not strange if they did so at
this campsite. But here they appear to have taken special pains
to make the rite as impressive as possible. There are some
plausible reasons for this. The huge semicircular rock with its
two widespread wings or arms may well have seemed reminiscent
of the chancel in their beloved churches far away across the sea.
Then, too, their arrival here may have coincided with the time

of a great feast day. The Feast of the Assumption of the Blessed Virgin comes on August 15th and, if the travelers left Hudson Bay about June 1st, they may have arrived at the rock about this time. It may also be that their somewhat elaborate festival was an expression of gratitude that their worst difficulties had been overcome. For many weeks they had labored hard, seeking a waterway leading eastward toward their headquarters in Vinland, but every river they came to led in the wrong direction. Now, at last, they had found a river which favored them. Joyful in its promise, it is reasonable to assume that they found a real pleasure in giving expression to their gratitude by creating, in this inviting spot, a semblance of the house of God in their homeland. And, as their priest stood before the altar arrayed in his full vestments, they must have sung their Te Deum Laudamus with more than customary fervor.

What is the meaning of these campsites and mooring stones?

The Kensington inscription tells of a voyage from Hudson Bay to a small lake in the west central part of Minnesota—a distance of more than a thousand miles. Only three points on this voyage are mentioned: (1) the place of beginning at Hudson Bay; (2) the place where the travelers left the inscribed stone; and (3) the place of massacre where they lost ten of their men.

But unconsciously they left many other marked stations. They camped preferably on the shore of a lake where there was the least danger of being surrounded and slaughtered by the enemy. Such a camp on the shore of a lake required a pier to which they could moor the boat, and an anchor for the other end. These "piers" were quickly made because they only required a hole drilled in a heavy boulder, a few inches deep. These thirteen mooring stones are found down through the lake park region of Minnesota, and we have the testimony of the first settlers that they were there when the first pioneers came. This is, therefore, excellent proof that a party of white men traveled through this region long before it was settled by white men.

In the next chapter it will be shown that this conclusion is corroborated by the discovery of more than a dozen weapons or other implements of the fourteenth century.

chapter fifteen

FOURTEENTH-CENTURY ARMS AND
IMPLEMENTS FOUND IN MINNESOTA

This research has been a lasting pleasure because of the continuous appearance of new and highly significant evidence. Most important of all was the discovery of the presence in Hudson Bay of Nicholas of Lynn and his group who proved to be identical with the ten men who, according to the Kensington inscription, were left in charge of the ships when the expedition divided.

Of almost equal importance was the discovery of fifteen campsites. The inscription mentions only one, where ten men were killed, but now we are able to follow the course of these travelers from the north end of Lake Winnipeg to the center of Minnesota, a distance of more than five hundred standard miles, by means of the mooring stones. These are stones that speak, and they all give the same message: "Here we were and spent the night!"

And now we have a third line of evidence—more than a dozen arms and implements from the late Middle Ages have been found. These artifacts have not been found scattered widely over America or even over Minnesota—nearly all were found in that small area marked by the mooring stones (see Figure 16). The presence of these relics antedates the arrival of the earliest pioneers because they were found by the pioneers when the latter began to till the soil. Furthermore, the metal in all of these finds has been analyzed by competent metallurgists and found to be of medieval origin, several hundred years old. Four of them were found on two campsites, and most of the

others have been found within ten miles of the route marked
by the mooring stones. This indicates that when the ten men
were attacked and killed at the Cormorant Lake campsite, most
of their equipment was seized by the savages.

The first of the artifacts to come to my attention was a
firesteel found in a layer of charcoal and ashes on the bank of a
former channel of Red River in Polk County, Minnesota (see
Figure 19). The following letter from the finder of this campsite
describes the circumstances clearly:

CLIMAX, MINN., June 8, 1914.

I have your letter concerning the firesteel which I found.
I settled here in June, 1871, and we were the first to take
land around here.

A short time after I settled here I was boring holes [for
fence posts] with a six-inch posthole auger. When I got
about two feet down I heard something scrape against the
auger and I pulled it up, thinking I had struck a stone.
The dirt clung to the auger, and I examined it looking for
the stone and found the little fire-steel. It was much rusted,
and there was also some charcoal and ashes. It must have
been there a long time, because the place where this hole
was bored was on a dry elevation.

OLE JEVNING

Firesteels were introduced early among the Indians, and
specimens may be seen in some museums. But it was found that
the firesteels brought in by the fur traders were different from
the one found by Ole Jevning. I wrote to the directors of a
dozen museums rich in Indian artifacts, but none had seen a
firesteel like it.

In 1928 I made an extensive trip through Europe for a
comparative study of this firesteel and other finds. Only in the
Scandinavian museums were there any such firesteels, and in the
University Museum in Oslo the Minnesota firesteel was immediately recognized as a Norse implement of the Viking age.
The museum kindly gave me the following statement identifying
the firesteel:

Upon request I will state that the firesteel which carries the [same identification] mark in its entire form, with the spiral ends, is of exactly the same type as the firesteels which have been found in Norwegian graves from the Viking age in great numbers.

OSLO, September 18, 1928.
EIVIND S. ENGELSTAD

There can be no doubt that this implement was left in its finding place hundreds of years ago, because it would take centuries for the dust of the prairie to cover the ashes of the campfire and the steel two feet deep. Before the prairie was plowed, there was very little dust, but as the firesteel was found just inside of the timber that lines the former channel of the river, what little dust there was would settle there, as the forest would check the wind. L. J. Young, Professor of Silviculture at the University of Michigan in a letter dated January 14, 1943, gives the following information on the precipitation of wind-borne dust particles when opposed by a forest:

When wind approaches a belt of trees, the velocity begins to decrease gradually to within about 100 feet of the windward edge of the belt. By the time the belt is reached, velocity is reduced to about 80%. At a distance of 50 feet or more inside of the belt, the velocity is reduced to about 2% and remains at about that level until the lee of the belt is reached.

The main channel of the Red River did not flow near the site of this camp in 1871, but had dug a new channel more than half a mile west of it. As the travelers would camp close to their boat in the river, this shift also indicates a great age because a forest centuries old now lies between the river and the campsite. Only at high water is there a small trickle on the east side of the old river bed which was covered by a big forest when I saw it in 1930.

Two other firesteels of the same type have been found. The small one (see Figure 19) was found in a crevice between two rocks at Cormorant Lake in 1870 by the first party of white men known to have visited this spot. In the university museum in Oslo may be seen several duplicates in size and ornamentation from the Middle Ages. The other, known as the Detroit Lakes firesteel, was found about twenty-five miles northeast of Detroit Lakes, Minnesota, by Otto Zeck, a local archaeologist, in a region not yet settled by white people. Nothing definite is known about its discovery, but as it is of the same type with spiralled ends, it was probably left by the same party of men. As these small firesteels were easily lost in the process of making fire, it is likely that more will turn up.

In addition to these firesteels, several axes, halberds, a spear, and two swords have been found. Most of these have been inspected by Dr. J. Bröndsted, Director of the National Museum in Copenhagen, who recognized all but one as authentic medieval implements. The most interesting of these finds are some small ceremonial halberds, of which at least three have been found. The first was found in 1871 by Mr. E. O. Estenson of Crookston, Minnesota, who is mentioned in the preceding chapter. Mr. Estenson, eighty-six years old when I interviewed him, made the find when he was eleven. The following is his own report:

CROOKSTON, MINN., Oct. 24, 1945.

The axe that you bought of Dr. Grassick was found by me in 1871 on the Dakota side of the Red River, opposite Frog Point where my father took a homestead the year before. The river-bank was eroding, and I saw the handle of the axe sticking out about two feet below the grassy surface of the bank. It was in the same battered condition, with a mineralized handle and broken blade, as it is now.[1]

E. O. ESTENSON

For further information, I sent the implement to the curators of five of the museums having the largest collections of Indian artifacts in the northern states; Milwaukee, Madison, St. Paul, Ann Arbor, and Toronto. Their answers were all to the effect that this implement was not a relic of the fur trade. Mr. Charles E. Brown of the Wisconsin Historical Society Museum wrote: "No such implement is listed in any of the fur trade invoices that I have seen. In its expensive construction it is unlike all other trade articles. Moreover the slender handle makes it worthless as an axe for Indian use. It looks to me like an ancient Norse weapon." (See Figure 21.)

The circumstances of these halberds *in situ* are such that they must have been in their finding places a long time before the coming of the first settlers. Mr. Estenson says in his letter above that his implement was found "two feet below the grassy surface of the top of the [eroded] bank." It must have taken hundreds of years for the winds of the prairie to build up two feet of soil above it. Great age is also indicated by the microscopic and spectrographic analysis to which the metal has been subjected, the results of such testing having definitely demonstrated that its metallurgy is not of a modern kind.

Another and emphatic evidence against the theory of importation by early settlers is the fact that this type of halberd is so rare that I have been unable to locate a single specimen in any of the Scandinavian museums. The likelihood that settlers may have come to America with so rare an item in their baggage, and that having once arrived here they immediately buried it at least two feet underground is too fantastic for serious consideration.

Sommerfelt and Knudsen describe it as follows: "The Norse halberd . . . of the 14th and 15th centuries had a long handle of wood which ended in a spear-head, and below this was an axe blade in the shape of a half moon. Opposite this was a pointed axe hammer." This is a good description of the Climax halberd even to the mention of the pointed axe hammer. It was also identified by Dr. Grieg, curator of the University Museum. He writes:

> Your letter of June 22, 1945, has been unanswered for some days as your inquiry necessitated some research. We find that the two halberds you sent us are without doubt of two halberds from the period around 1500.[2]
>
> University Museum
> SIGURD GRIEG

There is, however, one peculiarity about these halberds. The halberds of the Middle Ages were stout, effective weapons of warfare, but the Minnesota halberds are very small and light, the blade weighing only about a pound. As they were plainly too light for warfare, they must in all probability have been made for ceremonial usage. The halberd has always been the favorite ceremonial weapon. It is so used at present by the Swiss Guard at the Vatican, and it was used in the same way in former times. The *Century Dictionary* defines the word *Halberdier* thus: "A soldier of the bodyguard of a sovereign or high official. . . . The halberd was commonly borne by such attendants rather as an official badge than for actual service." Such a ceremonial halberd, of exactly the same shape, has been a part of the royal arms of Norway for many centuries.

We may therefore assume that, just as the Lictors of Rome carried the fasces as an emblem of consular authority on their errands to distant officials, so the members of King Magnus' bodyguard, who were his official representatives, carried this ceremonial weapon as a sign of royal authority. These artistically shaped ceremonial halberds with their graceful curves, their surfaces shining like polished silver, would be an ideal symbol of royal authority. As the king's mandate to Paul Knutson, the commander, states explicitly that the expedition was to consist in part of members of the king's bodyguard, the evidence accumulates that these ornamental halberds found in northwestern Minnesota were royal badges of King Magnus' bodyguard.

By accident the question of the authenticity of this and other halberds was confused by the fact that this emblem of royal authority in the fourteenth century was six hundred years later chosen to serve as a challenging symbol in a "cut-throat" tobacco advertising campaign. The American Tobacco Company, annoyed by competition, decided about 1890 to wage a "battle-axe" campaign for supremacy. The idea, it seems, was suggested by the discovery of one of these ceremonial halberds which was mistaken for a battle-axe, whereupon a "Battle-Axe Plug" was put on the market. Thousands of near-facsimile axes were made, hinged to a cutting-board to cut the plugs, and distributed to retail merchants (see Figure 22). Each plug was also provided with the battle-axe trademark. Later many of these tobacco cutters were converted into light axes by cutting off the hinged lever. These tobacco-cutting axes, of which there are still many in existence, are so closely similar to the Climax and other halberds that many think that they were all tobacco cutters. But while they are similar, their chemical structures are totally dissimilar. I asked Professor R. A. Ragatz, Chairman of the Department of Chemical Engineering, University of Wisconsin, to analyze the metal of one of the tobacco cutters. The following is his reply:

MADISON, WIS., February 22, 1945.

This letter pertains to the tobacco cutter patterned after a medieval halberd. I cut a small piece out of the frame (not the cutting blade) of the halberd part of the tobacco cutter, and made the following findings.

The metal is a rather poor quality of gray cast iron, showing the following micro-constituents: graphite plates, ferrite, pearlite, steadite. The structure is totally different from that shown by the frames of the two genuine halberds you sent me last fall. The frames of the two genuine halberds were made of malleable cast iron, and consisted of globular graphite and ferrite.

From my examination I can state positively that the two halberds sent me last fall were not of the same origin as the tobacco cutter recently submitted.

R. A. RAGATZ

It is easy to distinguish between an ancient ceremonial halberd, of which a number have been found in Minnesota, and a modern tobacco cutter. Figure 21 shows the pattern of the latter, and it will be noted that the upper point of the halberd has been converted into a hinge which, in the form of a snake-head, is connected with the base of the cutter. Those who wanted to change their tobacco cutter into a neat little axe were therefore obliged to saw off the snake-like hinge part. . . . The presence or absence of the saw marks therefore determines the age of the artifact.

THE REPUBLIC AXE

Another axe of indisputable age came to light a few years later outside of Minnesota. According to Morgan H. Stafford of Boston, Massachusetts, who obtained this axe shortly after it came to light, it was found in 1878 by a prospector in a wilderness near the present village of Republic in the northern peninsula of Michigan. He stooped down to take a drink from a stream. There, in the water, he saw an axe, but upon lifting it out of the water, the handle seemed to dissolve in his hand (see Figure 23).

Professor J. Bröndsted, who spent some weeks in America in 1948 for the purpose of investigating reported pre-Columbian Norse finds, thinks this is a Finnish axe. He was told that the Finns in Republic had similar axes which were used for squaring timbers. He therefore thinks it was a nineteenth-century product.

It is easy to be misled by a similarity. The axe is not Finnish but Norse, because I saw an *exact duplicate* in the Lillehammer museum in Norway. Moreover, it is a weapon and not a broadaxe as is shown by the fact that the outer end of the helve is protected by an iron "sleeve," five inches long, to prevent the head of the axe from being shorn off by an opponent's axe.

If this were all we knew about this find, I would not claim that this implement is evidence of the early presence of Norsemen in America. But the circumstances of the find put the matter in quite a different light. I borrowed the axe and sent it to Professor Darrah of Harvard, who was a recognized authority on vegetable microstructure. The following is his report made May 15, 1937:

> The wood in the handle of the axe found near Republic, Michigan is of subarctic spruce and might well have come from Norway or northern Canada, but not from as far south as the Great Lakes. It is significant that spruce is not strong or durable, and one can justifiably infer that spruce was used because other woods were scarce. The wood as now preserved in the axehead is dense, mineralized, and obviously decomposed. As to the reported fact that the protruding handle was decomposed to a paste-like substance,

it is my opinion that this indicates a submergence in water for several hundred years.

This set of conditions makes recent age out of the question.

W. C. DARRAH
Research Curator of Paleobotany
Botanical Museum of Harvard University.

This analysis by an expert produced three proofs that the implement was not a Finnish axe of the present time. First is Darrah's report on the great age of the handle—the "paste-like" condition of the handle indicating "a submergence in water for several hundred years." Secondly, the dense mineralized condition of the wood in the axehead which also indicates great age. Third, his statement that it is of subarctic spruce, not grown as far south as the Great Lakes. We must therefore visualize the owner of the axe as being so far north that the only available material for a handle was subarctic spruce. This brings us up to the vicinity of Hudson Bay. Later the axe was brought down to the region south of the international boundary. This happened several hundred years ago, as indicated by the pulpy condition of the handle and the mineralized condition of the wood in the axe-head. We have evidence of only one such journey from the subarctic region southward, and that is the one made by the company of eight Goths and twenty-two Norsemen who came from Hudson Bay southward in 1362 and reported their presence on the Kensington Stone.

The large axe found at Norway Lake (Figure 25), was a familiar object to most of the museum people with whom I talked, and was to be seen in several museums with minor differences. In the Kumla Church in Västmanland, Sweden, is a painting, showing the killing of King Olaf in 1030 (later known as Saint Olaf, see Figure 27). The painting dates from about 1450. Apparently the artist had no means of knowing just what kind of axes were used in the beginning of the eleventh century and used as a model the oldest axe he could find, which may have been a century old. As may be seen, while the two axes in this painting are identical in type, they show some minor differences. The following is the report of the man who found this axe:

NORWAY LAKE, MINN., July 30, 1908.

I hereby certify to the following facts:

In the summer of 1908, on one of my fishing trips to the peninsula projecting into Norway Lake . . . I came near the middle of said peninsula across an iron implement of peculiar shape. I picked it up and thought it must have been a part of a seeding machine or some other machinery; so I left it and went out on the lake fishing. . . .

During the following two years I saw articles in the newspapers about a remarkable stone found near Kensington. . . . The idea then occurred to me that possibly this axe on the peninsula had been one of the weapons of these Vikings. So, in the summer of 1910 I looked for it and found it and took it home. I have now loaned it to Hjalmar R. Holand.

OLE SKAALERUD

In presence of:
D. C. Jordan
P. A. Gundrud

The peninsula mentioned above was a part of the farm of Even Railson, the first settler (with his brother, Senator Andrew Railson) in Kandiyohi County. He never farmed this peninsula, but, being a good friend of the Indians, he permitted them to camp there. They were always given a hearty welcome.

Figure 24 shows a battle-axe found three miles southeast of Erdahl, Minnesota, or about fifteen miles northwest of Kensington. It weighs five and one-third pounds. The edge is eight and one-fourth inches long and the width of the axe from poll to edge is six and three-quarters inches. The eye of the axe is almost doubled in length by an addition below which may be called the neck, and is four and one-half inches long. This opening tapers considerably from the opening in the neck where it is quite big (one and seven-eighths by one and five-eighths inches) to the upper edge of the axe where it is quite small (one and one-eighth by one inch). The poll of the axe is superimposed by a hammerlike addition two and one-quarter by one and three-eighths inches in size and about one-quarter inch thick. The blade of the axe has a long downward extension.[3]

The reason this implement is called a battle-axe is that it is clearly not meant for chopping. The edge is like that of a crowbar, the blade being seven-eighths of an inch in thickness one and one-half inches from the edge. It is a little thicker at the lower point of the blade than at the upper. Most of the great weight of the axe is in the blade near the edge. It is therefore more a heavy maul than a tool for cutting. The only conceivable use it could have been put to is to smash helmets. Against a steel helmet, a spear or a sword would be harmless, being too light in the impact of the blow, but a blow from such a clublike axe, with the bulk of the weight near the edge, would smash any helmet if properly delivered. There is sufficient edge on this battle-axe not only to stun the opponent, but also to fracture the skull.

On one side of the axe (unfortunately not shown on the photograph) are two maker's marks. They are too much abraded to be deciphered. The following is an affidavit setting forth what is known of its finding.

MINNEAPOLIS, MINN., Dec. 11, 1928.

About thirty-five years ago my late husband, Julius Davidson, and I purchased a farm about five miles southwest of Evansville, Minnesota, and about three miles southeast of Erdahl. Being in need of more tillable land, Mr. Davidson in 1894 decided to clear and break up part of a piece of native woodland which was on the farm.

The trees had been cut some years before, and the stumps were pulled up by Mr. Davidson by means of a stump-puller. Beneath one of these stumps he found this heavy axe of strange shape, the like of which he had never seen before. The top of the stump under which the axe was found was more than two feet in diameter, and my husband said that it must have been several hundred years old. The axe lay quite deep in the hole, about a foot and a half below the surface of the ground. None of our neighbors had ever seen or heard of this axe before.

The axe was in my possession until last summer when I loaned it to Mr. H. R. Holand.

(Signed) MARTHA DAVIDSON

State of Minnesota,
County of Hennepin.

Subscribed and sworn to before me, a notary public, this 15th day of December, 1928.

(Signed) CHAS. A. PALMER

In 1928 I called on Dr. B. Thordeman, assistant curator of the Historical Museum in Stockholm, to see if he had any axe similar to the one described above. This museum, like the others, had very few arms from the period after the Viking Age, but it had a large number of reredoses from old churches. Dr. Thordeman pointed out a figure of King Olaf, who held in his hand an exact wooden image of the axe shown above in Figure 20. The size of the reredos and the lack of good light made it impossible to obtain a good photograph, but Dr. Thordeman gave me the following statement:

The axe marked B. Thm. [see Figure 24] is in type practically identical with St. Olaf's axe on the reredos from Österaker (originally from Storkyrkan in Stockholm), now in the National Historical Museum, dated 1468.

STOCKHOLM, Sept. 6, 1928.
(Signed) BENGT THORDEMAN

Figure 28 shows a sword found three miles west of Ulen in Clay County, Minnesota, in the spring of 1911 on the farm of Hans O. Hanson. He was a recent settler, but was the first to plow the soil on this farm. In an interview which I had with Mr. Hanson at the spot where the sword was found, he told me that he had plowed the field several times, but very shallow, as was the practice in that vicinity. Then, at a Farmer's Institute meeting, he had heard a speaker dwell on the benefits gained by deep plowing, and, much impressed, returned to his farm and set his plow point several inches deeper, It was then he turned up the sword, deeply incrusted with rust. He stated in his affidavit that he had spent much time removing the rust.

Rev. Horatio Gates, pastor of a church in Willmar, Minn., who accompanied me, secured affidavits from Mr. Hanson and his neighbors concerning the discovery of the sword and the settlement of the neighborhood. These affidavits brought out the fact that none of them had seen the sword before, nor had any knowledge of how it had come there. Unfortunately, these affidavits perished in 1934 when my house was destroyed by fire. The length of the blade at present is 16¼ inches, but originally it was longer, as it shows signs of having been cut off in a very crude manner. The bronze handle, including the cross-bar which served as hilt, is 6½ inches long and has spiral ornamentation.

This sword has some resemblance to the Roman style of swords which were used for a time in the U.S. Army in the early part of the nineteenth century. For this reason I wrote to the Smithsonian Institution to see if it had anything similar. The following is the reply of the Institution:

WASHINGTON, D. C., March 4, 1939.

Referring to previous correspondence and particularly to your letter of February 13, I regret to say that we have been unable to find any information whatever concerning the sword of which you submit a photograph.

Captain Charles Carey, Assistant curator of History, states that he will keep the specimen in mind, and we shall be glad to supply you with any information that we discover concerning it.

(Signed)   J. E. GRAF
Associate Director

There is one interesting point about this sword which indicates that it was not brought into Minnesota by immigrants or others in the nineteenth century. This is the manner in which a part of the sword has been cut off. Evidently the person who cut off the missing part did not have any cold-chisel, nor was there any blacksmith around. Instead, he set to work with a round-headed hammer to pound the blade in two. Not succeeding in this, he snapped off the piece desired. In so doing he fractured a corner of the remaining blade, which probably became thin by the pounding.

This indicates that an Indian was the blacksmith. If an Indian acquired it at Cormorant Lake, about twenty miles away, he would feel that his booty was not worth much because a sword is not an Indian weapon. But soon he would see that a part of the blade would make a good hunting knife, and he appears to have taken his stone-headed tomahawk to break the blade in two. The concave marks from the round head of the tomahawk are still visible for a distance of about 1½ inches on the remaining stub of the blade, and this has been flattened and widened by the impact of the blows.[3]

There is another remote possibility of how this sword may have reached this treeless prairie in the northern part of Minnesota. This is that it was brought in by a traveling group of players. But such groups would hardly have spent their time in such a thinly settled area as northwestern Minnesota, without any large villages or mining camps near by. Nor have the old settlers in or near Ulen any recollection of having seen any such "barn stormers." Finally, the finding place is far from any big road leading to Crookston, Grand Forks, or Winnipeg.

This sword could not have belonged to any later French or English trapper because, if they had carried swords at all, they would have been of the rapier type which came into use in the fifteenth century.

Figure 30 shows a wrought spearhead of steel, much pockmarked by rust. The point is seven inches long and 1½ inches wide at the widest part. A midrib is present, but not prominent. At the base of the blade is a conical socket 3½ inches long, into which the head of the shaft was introduced. The socket has two tongs or strap-like extensions of steel, ¹⁄₁₆ inch wide for securing the shaft. These tongs are 4¾ inches long, but were originally longer as the ends of both have been broken off. This weapon was found about forty miles east of the Mississippi in Trempealeau County, Wisconsin, in a small coulee among the steep ridges of Pigeon Creek. The land had been covered with timber and was recently cleared by the owner. It was while breaking up his first field that he found the spear among the roots of the clearing. The following affidavit gives an account of its discovery:

> I, Nils Windjue of Whitehall, Wisconsin, being under oath, make the following statement, to-wit:
>
> In the fall of 1899, while breaking up some new land on my farm in Sjuggerud Coulee, town of Pigeon, I found an ancient steel spearhead. It was actually found by my adopted son, George Windjue, then about five years old, who was playing about and saw the spearhead turned up by the breaking plow. . . . [Then follows a detailed description of the spearhead and the exact description of the place it was found.]
>
> (signed)   Nils Windjue

> Subscribed and sworn to before me, a notary public, in and for Trempealeau County, Wisconsin, on the 12th day of May, 1928.
>
> (Signed)   Chas. B. Melby

This was recognized in many museums as a true specimen of Scandinavian spears.

There remained the possibility that the spear is of English or other origin. A visit was therefore made to the Tower of London, where there is a large collection of spears. But I found that all the spears there are distinctly of another type, quite wide, with heavy midribs. They all have long shanks because the shaft is held in place by the shank only. The same is true of the German spears in the Zeughaus in Berlin. Neither the English nor the German or French spears have the strap-like tongs which are characteristic of Scandinavian spears. It is an error to suppose that "individual smiths have their own patterns." The shape of the spear, which in the Middle Ages was almost as much a part of a man's attire as a necktie is now, was prescribed by well-established national custom.

It now remains to ascertain if there is any coincidence between the route of the explorers, as marked by mooring stones, and the distribution of the old implements reported above. The

trail of a band of travelers is usually marked by various articles
which are left behind or lost on the way. Perishable articles
will, of course, soon disappear, but an iron weapon will remain
in the grass or timber until carried away. It is likely that some
of the articles would be picked up and carried away by Indians,
but, as every archaeologist knows, the greatest concentration of
artifacts is nearest to the point of distribution. If there is any
connection between the Norse implements and the mooring
stones, it is reasonable to expect that the finds would be centered
along the route traced above.

Of the thirteen or more medieval implements, nearly all
of which have been found under circumstances which exclude
the possibility that they were brought in by nineteenth-century
immigrants, nine have been found within twenty-five miles of
the route marked by the mooring stones. Four of these nine—
the Climax firesteel, the Climax halberd, the Cormorant Lake
firesteel, the Cormorant Lake axe—have been found right on
the waterway marked by the mooring stones.

Only two of these Norse artifacts have been found at any
considerable distance from Cormorant Lake where the massacre
took place and where most of these implements passed to the
hands of the Indians. These two are the Windjue spear and the
Republic axe. Both of these weapons are of a type familiar to
the Indians, and it is therefore likely that they were fought for
many times and carried far until they were finally lost.

In October, 1944, I was shown a peculiar little tool (see
Figure 31) found by Fred W. Krafthefer, an intelligent farmer,
whose address is Farwell, Minnesota. He told me he had found
it about six years earlier on a farm he then occupied, on the
east side of Lake Latoka, in the SE ½ of the NW ¼ of Section
26 in the township of LaGrande, about six miles southwest of
Alexandria, Minnesota. Lake Latoka is one of a connected string
of lakes which, together, make a navigable waterway across
southern Douglas County. Two mooring stones had been found
on this waterway, and I was looking for a third. Mr. Krafthefer
said he had shown the implement to many persons, but no one
had been able to tell what it could have been used for. It was

(and is) deeply honeycombed with rust, and was found near the shore of the lake.

As the illustration shows, the object consists of a cylindrical ring about the size and shape of a napkin ring. Attached to the middle of this ring, on the outside, is a quadrangular spike, $4\frac{1}{2}''$ long, which is perpendicular to the plane of the ring. The ring is about an inch wide and a little more than $1\frac{3}{4}''$ in diameter. The spike is $\frac{5}{16}''$ in diameter, but has probably lost some of its body by rusting. The end of the spike is not pointed. The nick in the ring was cut for microscopic study of the metal.

I followed Mr. Krafthefer's example and showed the implement to a large number of persons, including at least a dozen museum directors and workers who have more knowledge of strange and antique articles than most people, but I found no reasonable answer.

Upon request, Professor R. A. Ragatz, Chairman of the Department of Chemical Engineering, University of Wisconsin, kindly consented to make a microscopic study of the structure of the metal. He found that it differed from modern wrought iron in two respects. The following is his report, dated October 27, 1944:

> *Cylindrical Tool with Handle.* This material proved to be wrought iron. It is characterized by slag fibers surrounded by metal. The metal itself is largely iron (ferrite), though around the edges there has been some absorption of carbon with the resultant formation of pearlite. It is perfectly possible that this implement was made in medieval times, as the peoples of Europe in those days were well versed in the art of making wrought iron. The specimens differ from present-day wrought iron in two respects: (1) The ferrite is very impure. It shows what is known as a "cored structure," which is due to an uneven distribution of the phosphorus which is dissolved in the iron. (2) The outer regions were carburized, presumably with the idea of developing a harder surface condition than uncarburized material possesses. In present-day samples of wrought iron, I have not observed the intense "coring" shown by the sample being discussed. Furthermore, in present-day practice, no wrought iron articles are given a carburizing treatment.

In all probability, the wrought iron out of which the implement in question was fashioned was made by the direct reduction of ore with charcoal, without passing through the molten cast iron stage. The uneven phosphorus distribution points to that conclusion. The direct reduction process was the exclusive method of iron manufacture up till about 1340 A.D. While this approximate date marked the first production of molten cast iron, which was shortly followed by suitable processes for converting the cast iron into wrought iron, the old direct reduction process survived for hundreds of years but on an ever-declining scale. As a matter of fact, the last direct reduction furnace in the United States for making wrought iron shut down approximately in 1901.

The method of carburizing the surface of wrought iron was well known to medieval metal workers. While the process is not practiced today, no definite date may be set when it was no longer applied to wrought iron.

R. A. Ragatz

We have, then, three important premises which all point toward the conclusion that the implement is of ancient origin. These are: (a) It does not appear to have any modern use; (b) its metallurgical structure differs in two respects from that of modern wrought iron; (c) it was found within a few feet of a waterway over which the explorers of 1362 traveled. This suggests the possibility that it may have been brought in by these explorers. The question arises: Would they have any need of such an implement? While the evidence present is not as complete as might be desired, I think the answer is yes. The circumstances of their means of transportation would demand an implement of just this shape, size, and kind.

An inspection of the tool will show that the most reasonable function of the cylindrical part of the tool was to serve as a ferrule for a small pole or shaft. This assumption is supported by the fact that the interior of the ring is slightly convergent—the diameter of one side (opening) is about $\frac{1}{12}''$ larger than the other. This would appear to be for the purpose of facilitating solid wedging so that it would not slip off the pole. When the implement was thus affixed, it would resemble a pike pole, something like the pole implement used in directing the floating of logs. But this slender pike, only $5/16''$ in thickness, is too slender and too long for handling big logs. Furthermore, the end of the pike is blunt, so it was not used for thrusting or piercing. However, the explorers would need just such a tool, of precisely this shape, when mooring their boat, especially when there was some wave action.

In order to understand this need, it is necessary to have a clear idea of how the boat was moored. The mooring stone on the beach served as a pier to which the boat was fastened by means of a ringbolt or iron pin which fitted loosely into the hole in the stone. The boat could not lie in immediate contact with the rock, as the resultant friction would be injurious to the prow (or stern). In order to keep the boat from hammering against the rock, and also to keep it from swinging sidewise against the beach, it was necessary to anchor the outer end. In quiet weather this operation was an easy matter; but when the lake was rough, it was not so simple. In order to keep the boat from being thrown onto the beach, or swept sidewise by the waves, or pulled out by the undertow while the anchor was being dropped, it was necessary to hold the prow in position near the mooring stone. This could not be done by one of the crew clinging to the wet and slippery rock, but required a pike pole with a long and slender prong. By inserting this prong into the mooring hole as the boat approached the rock, the boat's motion could be controlled. It was necessary that the prong be straight and slender, because the mooring hole was small in diameter. It also had to be of good length to insure a good grip within the hole, so that it would not slip out as the boat heaved with the waves. The implement filled all these requirements perfectly.

In 1959 I presented all the Norse artifacts that I had collected to the Alexandria Museum where the Kensington Stone is. In this little museum are almost all the Scandinavian artifacts dating from the late Middle Ages found in America. The Luther College Norwegian Museum is a very fine museum, much larger than the Alexandria museum, but it has only one artifact, an axe from the fourteenth century. This, too, should be in the Alexandria museum because this axe was found at Cormorant Lake.

In 1960, after this chapter was written, reports came of the discovery of three new finds. One (Figure 29) is a sword of the same type as the Ulen sword (see Figure 28), but the crossbar is missing. A piece of the blade was sent to Professor David J. Mack, Chairman of the Department of Metallurgical Engineering, University of Wisconsin, and he made the following report on the sword August 17, 1960. "This structure consists of a high carbon wrought iron sword, a most unusual material which has not been made (to my knowledge) since the introduction of crucible steel two hundred years ago. This is a material which was used extensively by medieval armourers."

The finder, Andrew Stene, is now living in Pennock, Minn. It was found thirty or forty years ago, about two miles west of Brooten, Pope County, Minnesota, while plowing a spot on his farm which had not previously been plowed because it was close to an old fence.

The second find was a ceremonial halberd of exactly the same shape and size as those described above, but in a much better state of preservation. It was found in September, 1946, on a farm near Mt. Vernon in southeastern South Dakota "near the edge of grass slough." The owner is Richard D. Knox, Mt. Vernon, South Dakota.

I sent the Knox halberd to Professor Mack, and the following is his report:

October 31, 1960.

I appreciate the opportunity of examining the ceremonial halberd which you sent me. One small piece was removed from the cutting edge and another from the edge of the socket into which the wooden handle was inserted. Both pieces are covered with a fairly thick layer of "mill scale" which is the oxide FeO. This heavy coating accounts for the excellent state of preservation. Such a coating can only be produced at elevated temperature, 800-1000° F. and hence

I conclude that the halberd went through a fire. The temperature could not have been much above this, otherwise the microstructure would have been changed.

The blade is a good quality steel containing about 0.6% carbon, but it has not been hardened by heating and quenching. It is in what we call the annealed state, meaning it was cooled rather slowly from high temperature. It puzzles me that a medieval armorer who could produce such an excellent quality steel did not harden it further.

The remainder of the halberd is a rather dirty nonuniform wrought iron which is a typical medieval material. On the whole, I feel it is probably an ancient halberd, certainly 150-200 years minimum. While I feel it is ancient, I would hesitate to say how it got here, although I believe you are absolutely correct in your feeling about the pre-Columbian vikings. There is sufficient carbon in the blade to permit radio-carbon dating if Mr. Knox would be willing to sacrifice half the blade. . . .

Sincerely
DAVID J. MACK

The last of these medieval implements to come to my attention is the so-called Mora axe (see Figure 25). I am indebted to Dr. O. B. Overn, President of Concordia College, St. Paul, Minnesota, for information and scientific report about this axe. The following is his report to me.

May 10, 1961

The ax was found in 1933 by Mr. William H. Williams on his farm eight miles south of Mora in Kanabec County, Minnesota, while he was cutting corn. His address was Ogilvie, Minn. and his farm was SE of SE of Sec. 22—T. 38 —R 24. The ax was found about 20 rods NW of the buildings. He was accompanied by Thomas Williams when he found the ax. Mr. Williams is now deceased. He kept the ax in his home until Dec., 1936, when it passed into the hands of Rev. H. C. Jaus of Mora. Rev. Jaus was a great collector and recognized the unusual character of this ax. He traded a very large Australian fiery opal for it. Rev. Jaus was getting old and decided to give a large part of his collection to Concordia College which he did early in 1937. Thus the ax came into the possession of the Concordia College Museum. As director of the museum I have had custody of the ax since that time.

During the years, 1937 and 1938, Prof. R. L. Dowdell of the School of Mines of the University of Minnesota made some metallurgical tests of the ax at my request. These showed an exceedingly low carbon content in the wedge, probably less than .05%. This means that it is wrought iron of a composition that has not been used in axes during the last two centuries. The blade contains considerable slag. It is probable that it has been made from puddled iron which has been carburized and the blade welded into the ordinary wrought iron of the wedge. The hardness of the blade is far below that of modern axes. Its microscopic structure shows troostite which indicates that the blade was quenched in some type of solution for the tempering treatment.

O. B. OVERN

chapter sixteen

ANOTHER RUNIC INSCRIPTION

In addition to the many arms, implements and literary remains which bear witness to the presence of a Norse expedition in America in the fourteenth century, there also appears to have been another runic inscription. This was found in 1738 in the central part of North Dakota by Captain Pierre de La Verendrye, the first white man reported to have visited that state.

La Verendrye, one of the greatest of the French explorers of America, was born at Three Rivers on the St. Lawrence in 1685. In his youth he served for several years as an ensign on the battlefields of France. Later he was commandant of a fur-trading post on Lake Nipigon, the most distant of all French frontier posts. Here the lure of the great mysterious West seized him and he determined to explore its unknown wilds, partly to add new provinces to the French dominion and partly to search for a short and feasible route to the Pacific Ocean. He applied to the king for support in this great enterprise, but was only granted permission to undertake the expedition at his own expense. In 1731 he set out from Quebec with fifty men after turning all his resources and credit into cash. The following year he reached the western shore of Lake of the Woods on the boundary between Minnesota and Manitoba. Here he built his headquarters, Fort St. Charles, and pushing out to the west and north built several other frontier forts. Years of distress and disaster followed, caused by the failure of supplies to arrive, the mutiny of his men, and the attacks of the Sioux Indians. But with dauntless perseverance and resourcefulness, La Verendrye maintained his hold on the region and extended the dominion of France in every direction.

He heard strange stories from the Indians of a nation of

white people who were not hunters but agriculturists, living far
to the southwest. In 1738 he made a journey to this strange
people and found them to be the Mandan Indians, occupying
between the present cities of Minot and Bismarck, North
Dakota. Somewhere in this area he discovered a pillar of stone
in which was fixed a small stone inscribed on both sides with
unknown characters. He was unable to decipher the inscription
but it was most precious to him and he kept it for five years,
and then in 1743 he took it with him to Quebec. He submitted
it to the scrutiny of the Jesuit scholars there. They were likewise
unable to read the inscription; but on comparing it with illustrations of Tatarian inscriptions which they found in books in
their college library, they found the characters "perfectly alike."
Esteeming this discovery a matter of state importance, the stone
with its mystic inscription was sent to Paris to Count de Maurepas, Minister of Colonies.

The record of this remarkable discovery is preserved to us
by Professor Peter Kalm, a member of the Swedish Royal
Academy of Sciences, who about that time was sojourning in
America. While here he kept a diary of his observations which
later was published in three volumes.[1] In 1749 he visited Quebec,
where he not only heard the story of the discovery of this
inscribed stone from the Jesuit scholars in the city, but also
received an account of it from Captain La Verendrye himself
who happened to be there. The account that Professor Kalm
gives of it is therefore practically firsthand. The following is
Kalm's report about the matter:

> The history of the country can be traced no further than
> from the arrival of the Europeans; for everything that
> happened before that period, is more like a fiction or a
> dream, than anything that really happened. In later time
> there have, however, been found a few marks of antiquity,
> from which it may be conjectured that America was former-
> ly inhabited by a nation more versed in science, than that
> which the Europeans found on their arrival here; or that a
> great military expedition was undertaken to this continent,
> from these known parts of the world.

This is confirmed by an account, which I received from

Mr. de Verandrier, who has commanded the expedition to the South Sea [the Pacific] in person, of which I shall presently give an account. I have heard it repeated by others, who have been eye-witnesses of everything that happened on that occasion. Some years before I came into Canada, the then governor-general, Chevalier de Beauharnois, gave Mr. de Verandrier an order to go from Canada, with a number of people, on an expedition across North America to the South Sea, in order to examine how far those places are distant from each other, and to find out what advantages might accrue to Canada or Louisiana, from a communication with that ocean. . . . As they came far into the country, beyond many nations, they sometimes met with large tracts of land, free from wood, but covered with a kind of very tall grass, for the space of some days' journey. . . . At last they met with a large stone, like a pillar, and in it a smaller stone was fixed, which was covered on both sides with unknown characters. This stone, which was about a foot of French measure in length, and between four or five inches broad, they broke loose, and carried to Canada with them, from whence it was sent to France, to the secretary of state, the Count of Maurepas. What became of it afterwards is unknown to them, but they think it is yet (1749) preserved in his collection. Several of the Jesuits, who have seen and handled the stone in Canada, unanimously affirm, that the letters on it are the same with those which in the books, containing accounts of Tataria, are called Tatarian characters, and that, on comparing both together, they found them perfectly alike.

It is evident from this account that this inscribed stone was not an Indian pictograph. Pierre de La Verendrye had spent more than fifty years in Canada,[2] mostly among the Indians, and probably had seen dozens of such pictographs. The Jesuits of Quebec, likewise, many of whom had spent years among the Indians as missionaries, were also familiar with their pictographs. Indeed, the picture writing of the Indians has so little in common with the appearance of the writing of more civilized peoples, that even one who sees it for the first time would not confuse it with the alphabetic characters of any other people. Professor

Kalm states that the Jesuits, upon comparing the writing on the stone with illustrations of Tatarian inscriptions found the characters "perfectly alike." This comparison is helpful, but of course, it could not have been a Tatarian inscription, for the Tatars, living east of the Caspian Sea, with no known interest in seafaring and exploration, would be among the last peoples on earth to have found their way into the interior of North America.

It happens, however, that Tatarian inscriptions and runic inscriptions have a remarkable superficial resemblance. This has already been noted by Sir Charles Eliot who in his article in the *Encyclopaedia Britannica* on Turks calls attention to this resemblance.[3] The letters in both modes of writing are most often formed on a vertical staff and they are mostly rectangular in form. Several runic signs have their duplicates in Tatarian characters which occur in inscriptions on the upper Yenesei and Orkhon rivers. The similarity of runic and Tatarian inscriptions is shown in the illustration of a Tatarian inscription (see Figure 38).[4]

As the Jesuit scholars found these characters in an illustrated book on the Tatars, it may be possible to get a definite image of Verendrye's inscription by consulting the illustrated books on Tatars that were published before 1743. While several books on the Tatars were published before this date, there was only one, according to the Librarian of Congress, which shows specimens of Tatar writing. This is Philipp Johann von Strahlenberg's *Das Nord- und Östliche Theil von Europa und Asia,* published in German in Stockholm, 1730, 4to. Strahlenberg was a Swedish officer who for thirteen years had been a captive among the Tatars, and his book was by far the most popular of its kind, being translated and published in many editions, among them being an English translation in 1736, another in 1738, and a French in 1757. The first or second of these must therefore have been the book on the Tatars in which the Jesuit scholars in 1743 found illustrations of writing "perfectly like" the writing on the Verendrye stone. In view of the fact that only an expert in runic or Tatarian writing would be able to distinguish between the two, there seems to be good reason to believe that La

Verendrye found a runic inscription. This conclusion is strengthened by the fact that it was found near the same region in the Northwest which Norsemen, possessing the knowledge of runes, are reported to have visited. Its position, when found, on top of a large stone or pillar, was duplicated by the Norsemen who about 1300 reached the 73rd parallel in Greenland, where they built a beacon or cairn of stone and wrote their inscription upon a smaller stone which they placed upon it.

It is possible to limit greatly the field in which the pillar with the inscribed stone was found. Kalm states in the beginning of his account that the Verendrye with whom he talked in 1749 was in personal command of the expedition on which they found the inscribed stone. This excludes the three sons, for they were all in the West in 1749. La Verendrye *père* must therefore have been the Verendrye with whom Kalm talked. Now we know from the elder La Verendrye's own published account that he did not personally penetrate farther west than the first Mandan village somewhere in the northern part of McLean County, North Dakota.

This mystic inscription was sent to Count de Maurepas and probably baffled the count and his advisers as much as it had bewildered the learned Jesuits in Quebec. While something was known of Tatarian inscriptions, the day of runic interpretation had not yet arrived.

There is considerable evidence indicating that the Mandans had been in long contact with Christian white people before they were visited by La Verendrye in 1738. But as this subject lies beyond the scope of this book, it is here omitted. In *Westward From Vinland*, pp. 263-86, published by Duell, Sloan and Pearce, New York, I have a chapter on this subject.

chapter seventeen

THE END OF THE TRAIL

It is very fitting that a runic inscription should be found in the central part of North Dakota because there, in the land of the Mandans, was the last home of the men who inscribed the Kensington Stone.

The Mandans are the greatest enigma in the study of the North American Indians. Unlike other Indian tribes who were nomadic hunters, the Mandans lived in large and well fortified towns in roomy dwellings of relatively permanent construction, and subsisted chiefly by agriculture. Most remarkable is the fact that they were of mixed origin, many individuals among them being almost white in color. Moreover, their traditions showed strong reminiscences of association with white people, and their customs and religious beliefs were largely of a Christian character. Our knowledge of them goes back about 230 years, which was about 150 years before the first pioneers came there.

The widespread reports of the advanced culture of the Mandans and their strange characteristics early caused many travelers to visit them.[1] Captain Pierre La Verendrye, the first Frenchman known to have penetrated into the region west of the upper Mississippi in Minnesota, was the first of these. In 1732, after pushing hundreds of miles beyond the farthest earlier advance, he built a fort on the west side of Lake of the Woods. During the following years, in which he was preparing to seek a way to the Pacific, he heard from the Indians many strange tales of a people farther west who were said not to be Indian but white people like himself. In 1738 he therefore set out on a journey of several hundred miles to visit these people. He found the Mandans, comfortably settled in six large villages on the Missouri, some distance southwest of the present city of Minot,

North Dakota. His hope of meeting countrymen was quickly
dispelled when he arrived in the first village, but he was never-
theless deeply impressed with the fact that he had here reached
a tribe very different from those he had previously seen in his
lifetime among the Indians. The following is a part of his
description of this Mandan village.

Mr. de la Marque and I walked about to observe the size
of their fort and their fortifications. I decided to have the
huts counted. It was found that there were 130 of them.
All the streets, squares and huts resembled each other.
Several of our Frenchmen wandered about; they found the
streets and squares very clean, the ramparts very level and
broad; the palisades supported on cross-pieces morticed
into posts of fifteen feet to twice fifteen feet. There are
green skins which are put for sheathing where required,
fastened only above in the places needed, as in the bastion
there are four at each curtain well flanked. The fort is
built on a height in the open prairie with a ditch upwards
of fifteen feet deep by fifteen or eighteen feet wide.[2] Their
fort can only be gained by steps or posts which can be
removed when threatened by an enemy. If all their forts
are alike, they may be called impregnable to Indians. Their
fortifications are not Indian. This nation is mixed white
and black. The women are fairly good-looking, especially
the white, many with blond and fair hair. Both men and
women of this nation are very laborious; their huts are
large and spacious, separated into several apartments by
thick planks; nothing is left lying about; all their baggage
is in large bags hung on posts; their beds made like tombs
surrounded by skins. . . . Their fort is full of caves (caches)
in which are stored such articles as grain, food, fat, dressed
robes, bear skins. They are well supplied with these; it is
the money of the country. . . . The men are stout and tall,
generally very active, fairly good-looking, with a good physiognomy. The women have not the Indian physiognomy.
The men indulge in a sort of ball play on the squares
and ramparts.[3]

The following is a list of Mandan characteristics as shown
in their fortifications, dwellings, historical tradition, complexions

and religious beliefs, which are not only different from those of all other Indian tribes but indicate that at some remote time they had been in close contact with white people.

1. Fortifications. These have been described above. As La Verendrye visited the Mandans about 150 years before Dakota had any white settlers, this shows that they must have learned to build these fortifications at a very remote time.

2. Dwellings. The Mandans lived in large round houses, forty feet or more in diameter. George Catlin, who was a good artist, was a guest in one of these round houses for several weeks, and while there he made a drawing of it from the inside which shows how it was constructed. The entire house was covered with a layer of clay a foot or more thick.

Similar round houses were in use in some parts of Norway in the Middle Ages. We have a description of one by Captain Pietro Quirini, a Venetian sea captain, who was shipwrecked in 1432 on or near the island of Röst in northern Norway.[4] He and his surviving men spent the winter in such a round house differing only from a Mandan house in the more abundant use of timber. This difference was probably due to the fact that the Mandans had no good axes.

3. By far the most important historical tradition among the Mandans was the coming of the white men. In each Mandan village was a symbolical canoe, in memory of the time long ago when the first white man came to them from the west and taught them how to become great people. It represented the aspirations he had planted in the national consciousness, and this aspiration had grown so big that it became a tribal renaissance which enabled them to grow in ethical stature long after he had passed away.

According to their tradition, this white man came from the *west*, which may seem erroneous because Europe lies far to the east. But when the surviving members of the explorers who left the Kensington inscription reached the Mandans, they were actually travelling eastward. Their course had been southward until they reached Barrett Lake in Grant County. But here they found a waterway leading east, as may be seen on the map printed in this book. According to old traditions mentioned in the *Handbook of American Indians*,[5] the earlier habitat of the Mandans was in eastern Minnesota and northwestern Wisconsin; and here, not far from the end of the chain of mooring stones, is probably the place where the two groups met and united.

4. All the many writers from Verendrye's time down to comparatively recent years who have visited the Mandans are agreed that the Mandans were a mixed tribe of Indians and white men (see note 1). There were many individuals, especially among the women, with blue, hazel or gray eyes and various colors of hair except white or red. Maximilian, who was a careful observer, says: "After a thorough ablution the skin of some of them appears almost white, and even some color in their cheeks." He also says that "the noses of the Mandans were less aquiline than those of other Indians and they have less prominent cheek bones."

When George Catlin was on his way to visit the Mandans, he was told by Governor William Clark that he would find a "half white" nation. As Mr. Clark had spent the entire winter of 1804-5 with the Mandans, he was in position to know.

The suggestion may occur to some readers that these light-colored people were albinos, but this would be an erroneous conclusion. An albino is one who is suffering from a congenital deficiency of pigment in the skin, and is thin, weak and morbid. Albinos have white hair and the iris of their eyes is pink. They suffer from strong lights, and sunlight almost blinds them.

5. Religious beliefs.

Captain Verendrye, in his report of his visit to the Mandans in 1738 (which was not published until almost a hundred years later), says nothing about the traditions and religious belief of the Mandans because he lost his interpreter the day after he arrived there. Nor were there any other visitors there for many years. But about 1782 some French missionaries visited them and to their surprise and joy found a tribe of Christian Indians. There is no copy of their report, but the substance of it is printed in the *Pennsylvania Packet* and *General Advertiser* of August 26, 1784. It reads as follows:

> Letters from Boston mentions that a new nation of white people has been discovered about 2,000 miles beyond the

Appalachian Mountains. They are said to be acquainted with the principles of the Christian religion and to be exceedingly courteous and civilized. This account was brought by the Indians to Boston, and concurs with others which were reported by two French missionaries at Montreal last year.

This was some years before any trading post was built among or near the Mandans. In 1784, The Northwest Fur Company was organized, and a few years later it established a trading post near the Mandans.

Most Indians believed that all manifestations of nature, such as rivers, trees, winds, animals, etc., had spirits which were not essentially good or bad, but could be persuaded by prayers and gifts of tobacco to take a favorable attitude toward the beseeching Indians. The Mandans, however, had the Christian concept of the evil-minded Devil, always busy stirring up trouble.

They also had traditions of a young man *born of a virgin* who was a worker of miracles. Once he saved the entire tribe from death by starvation. The crops had failed, and the game disappeared. Then the young man went out and killed four buffalo bulls. These were cut up and given to the people—leaving as much meat as there was before they had eaten.[6]

In the Mandan tradition this feeding of the multitude is by buffalo meat instead of bread and fish as in the gospel narrative. According to Catlin and Maximilian, buffalo meat was the choicest food to the Mandans. It is quite feasible that if they had heard of the miracles of Jesus, this miracle of the feeding of the multitude would be the one to make the deepest impression upon them—for, indeed, such was the case in Palestine where it was first told. This miracle is the only one which is related by all four gospel writers.

Summarizing the results of the above study, we have the following facts:

a) The Mandans were partly descended from white people.

b) These people had blue eyes, fair hair and were Christians.

c) They had come across the sea in a *big canoe*.

d) The Mandan house in its structural type, roof covering and material is different from the types of dwellings used by other tribes in America, but is similar to Norse houses in the late Middle Ages.

e) They were, as the missionaries said, acquainted with the principles of the Christian religion.

f) Near a Mandan village, Captain Verendrye found a stone containing an inscription which apparently was runic.

Just how these white men came to amalgamate with the Mandans we cannot say. Perhaps a remnant of the Mandans was at that time fleeing from their enemies the Sioux and met the Norsemen. As the latter had also lost many men to the Sioux, they may have found it expedient to seek safety in a more sparsely settled region. Though small in numbers, this community, by reason of the intelligence and experience of its white leaders, was able to defend itself so well in recurring attacks that it eventually became a large one well entrenched in fortified towns, as was the case when they were visited by Captain Verendrye in 1738.

NOTES

CHAPTER ONE

1. *Grönlands Historiske Mindes,* III, 259. See also, Jon Duason in *Landkönnum og Landnam Islendinga i Vesturheimi,* p. 170 and A. A. Björnbo in *Cartographia Groenlandica.*
2. G. Storm, *Islandske Annaler,* p. 354.
3. *Grönlands Historiske Mindes,* II, 459-64.
4. *Det Norske Folks Historie, Unionsperioden,* I, 314.

CHAPTER TWO

1. A photostat copy is printed in William Thalbitzer's *Two Runic Stones from Greenland and Minnesota,* translated and published by the Smithsonian Institution, *Miscellaneous Collections,* Vol. 116, No. 3.
2. *Studier over Vinlandsreiserne,* 1888, pp.73-75.
3. *Historia de gentibus septentrionalibus* (Rome, 1555), II, 92.
4. By previous agreement King Magnus yielded the throne of Norway to his son King Haakon when the latter reached his majority in August, 1355. However, some districts, including the greater part of West Gothland which belonged to his queen, were retained by King Magnus.
5. Claudius Clavus on one of his maps of the following century says that two other Eskimo boats were hung in the Trondheim Cathedral.
6. P. A. Munch, *Det Norske Folks Historie, Unionsperioden,* II, 106.

CHAPTER THREE

1. Printed in *Minneapolis Journal,* February 22, 1899. *Symra,* a Norwegian American literary quarterly, published in Decorah, Iowa, contains Breda's own defense in the issue of 1910, Vol. 6, 65-80.
2. *Skandinaven,* March 3, 1899.
3. H. R. Holand, *The Kensington Stone,* 1932, pp. 124-28.
4. *Speculum,* July, 1950, 324

CHAPTER FOUR

1. The book was published in 1908, a volume of more than six hundred pages. As the pioneers had not yet gained a knowledge of English, I wrote the book in Norwegian, so that the pioneers could see that we appreciated their great work. It had an excellent reception and was published in five editions. It was the first comprehensive history of the Norwegian-American immigration up to the Civil War.

2. The report is printed in full in the *MHS Collections,* XV, 238-40. Also in Holand, *The Kensington Stone,* 1932, pp. 276, 277.

3. A more detailed report on Sven Fogelblad is printed in Holand, *The Kensington Stone,* 1932, pp. 284-87.

CHAPTER FIVE

1. The exact date within two or three days is debatable.

2. Wahlgren, in his book, *The Kensington Stone,* p. 80, says there were forty men in this sub-expedition, but the inscription says thirty ("8 Goths and 22 Norsemen"). Twenty men went inland and ten men were left with the ships.

3. Wahlgren, p. 74.

4. Wahlgren, p. 74.

5. Quaife is wrong in saying that the Nelson is ice-locked until July. *The Hudson Bay Pilot* (1954) p. 315, says: "The rivers and roads outside are free of ice by the middle of June" and again, "the river ought to be safe for navigation from June 15 until Dec. 1st."

6. F. Nansen, *In Northern Mists,* II, 170 n. 1; G. M. Gathorne-Hardy, *Norse Discoverers of America,* 1921, pp. 196-211; W. Hovgaard, *The Voyages of the Norsemen to America,* 1914, pp. 61-64; A. Fossum, *The Norse Discovery of America,* pp. 80, 91.

CHAPTER SIX

1. Dr. Hoegh's report is printed in *Symra,* a quarterly in Decorah, Iowa, 1909, 178-89.

2. *Svenska Amerikanska Posten,* Minneapolis, May 23, 1899.

3. MHS Report, in *Collections,* Vol. 15, p. 222.

4. George T. Flom, *The Kensington Rune-Stone*, 1910, p. 4.

5. Photographs of these cross-sections, slightly reduced because of page limitations, are printed in MHS Report, 1909-14, Vol. 15, plates IV and V. Also in Holand, *The Kensington Stone*, 1932, opposite pages 38-40.

6. H. R. Holand, *The Kensington Stone*, 1932, p. 40.

7. Dr. Hoegh's report on the Kensington Stone is printed in *Symra*, Decorah, Iowa, 1909, 178-79.

8. Wahlgren, *The Kensington Stone*, p. 35.

9. Wahlgren, p. 43.

10. Wahlgren, pp. 36-38.

11. Wahlgren, pp. 40, 41.

12. *Symra*, Decorah, Iowa, V, 187.

13. G. T. Flom, "The Kensington Rune Stone," publication of Illinois Historical Society, No. 15, 1910, p. 106.

14. *Catholic Church in St. Paul*, 1952, p. 7.

15. "The Kensington Stone," Preliminary Report to the Minn. His. Soc. Second Ed. printed in *Minn. Soc. Collections*, Vol. 15, p. 268.

16. *Ibid.*, p. 286.

17. *Ibid.*, p. 105.

18. Wahlgren, p. 44. On p. 175 he has a similar statement; he says: "It is quite likely that the actual carving had not been performed by then (1897)."

19. *Symra*, 1909, p. 186.

20. *Minn. Hist. Society's Committee Report, Collections*, 1915, p. 225.

21. F. J. Pohl, *Atlantic Crossings Before Columbus*, 1961, p. 223.

CHAPTER SEVEN

1. Wahlgren, *The Kensington Stone*, p. 61.

2. *MHS Report*, pp. 235-36.

3. *MHS Report*, pp. 221, 233, 246, 248.

4. *Records of the Past*, Vol. IX, 1910.

5. "*The Kensington Stone*," an address by George T. Flom. Ill. *State Historical Society*, 1910, pp. 106, 107.

6. Letter of February 25, 1952.

8. *MHS Report*, p. 233.

8. *Journal of American History*, (1910), IV, 180.

9. Wahlgren, p. 66. The disintegration of the upper edge of the incised lines, as noted by Professor Curme (see below), would not be affected by this cleansing process.

10. Statement on file in the archives of the Minn. Hist. Soc.

11. *Skandinaven*, Chicago, March 3, 1899. In my *Explorations in America Before Columbus*, the date of the issue is given as May 3. This is a misprint.

12. From letter of December 9, 1960.

CHAPTER EIGHT

1. "Problemet om Nordboer i Nordamerika för Columbus" in *Aarbog for Nordisk Oldk. og Historie*, 1950, pp. 70, 141.

2. *Ibid.*, p. 86.

3. *The Physical Geography of Wisconsin*, 2nd edition, 1932, p. 464.

4. *Journal of American History*, 1910, IV, 180.

CHAPTER NINE

1. It is fully discussed in Holand, *The Kensington Stone*, 1932, pp. 257-59.

2. Fritzners *Ordbog*, 1886, article *man*.

3. *Svensk Dipl. Förste Smling*, No. 4503.

4. S. N. Hagen, "The Kensington Runic Inscription" *Speculum*, 1950, XXV, 329.

5. Axel Kock, *Svensk Ljudhistoria*, 1906, II, 38-42.

6. *Dipl. Norw*, IV, No. 586. The original is preserved.

7. G. T. Flom, "The Kensington Rune-Stone," *Transactions of the Illinois Historical Society*, May 10, 1910, pp. 26-30.

8. Holand, *The Kensington Stone*, 1932, pp. 119-24.

9. Flom, *Ibid.*, pp. 13, 16-18.

10. *Speculum*, July, 1950, p. 328.

11. See his book, pp. 133ff.

12. *Norsk Språkhistorie til omkning 1370*, 1931, p. 249. See also Magnus Olsen in "Kingigtorsoak-Stenen," *Norsk Tidsskrift for Sprogvidenskab*, 1932, V, 240, 241.

13. Falk and Torp, *Dansk Norskens Syntaks* 1900, 164, 2. M. Nygaard, "Subjektlöse Sætninger i det Norrone Sprog." *Arkiv f. Nordisk Filologi*, 1894, pp. 1-16.

14. *Västgötalagan,* Collin and Schlyter's Ed. 1827, *Corpus* 1, pp. iv and v.

15. Joseph Wright, *Historical German Grammar,* p. 42. From the Germans came also the suffix *else* in such words as *opfarelse, opstañdelse, optagelse,* etc., which all occur in *Västgötalagen,* Ms. 1285. See H. R. Holand, *The Kensingtone Stone,* p. 232.

16. *Dip. Nor. I,* No. 409.

17. Wahlgren, *The Kensington Stone,* p. 109.

18 See L. M. Hollander in *Scandinavian Studies,* Nov. 1949, p. 184.

19. P. A. Munch, *Unionsperioden,* Vol. 1, pp. 596, 373. See also Amund B. Larsen in *Arkiv f. Nor Filologi,* 1897, p. 244.

20. *Dansk-Norskens Syntaks,* 1900, pp. xii, xiii.

21. *Norsk Tidsskrift for Sprogvidenskap,* VII, 220.

22. *Dansk-Norskens Syntaks,* 1900, pp. xiii, xiv.

23. "Litt um Burtfallet av Flertall i Verbalböygjingi i Norsk" in *Festskrift til Amund B. Larsen* 1924, pp. 106-14.

24. Arkiv f. Nordisk Filologi, 1918, pp. 127ff.

25. Wahlgren, p. 114.

26. For other examples of its use, see Fritzner's or Vigfusson's dictionaries.

27. *Information,* Copenhagen, Nov. 9, 1949.

28. *Speculum,* 1950, p. 340.

29. Wahlgren p. 109.

CHAPTER TEN

1. Page 61, (Wahlgren, *The Kensington Stone,* p. 146, Fig. 22).

2. A brief but lucid explanation of the runic numerals is given in von Friesen's excellent work, *Runorna i Sverige,* 1928, pp. 82-84. According to Professor Sophus Bugge, *Norges Indskrifter med de eldre Runer,* II, 499, the use of these runic *primstaver* goes back as far as the beginning of the fourteenth century.

3. *Annaler for Nor. Oldkyndighed,* 1848, pp. 353-75.

4. *Svensk Familjebok,* Article *J.*

5. *Nordisk Kultur,* Vol. 6, p. 8; Kock in *Svensk Ljudhistoria,* II, 284.

6. Lauritz Nielson, *Danmarks Middelalderlige Haandskrifter,* 1937, p. 97.

7. See excellent facsimiles in Reeves, *The Finding of Wineland the Good*, pp. 144, 147.

8. Josep Wright, Historical German Grammar, p. 42. Adolph Noreen, *Nordisk Familjebok*, Vol. 34, article o. "In Middle High German the sign ö was used to represent the ö sound."

9. A. Taranger, *Norges* Historie, Vol. III, Part 1, p. 144.

10. *Information*, Copenhagen, Nov. 9, 1949.

11. *Danske Studier*, 1950, pp. 45-47.

12. *Ibid.*, p. 42. Hugo Jungner has photographed and described 113 runic inscriptions in West Gothland, Sweden. 95 have the same rune for *n* as appears on the Kensington Stone. Only 18 have the sign 1. See his *Västergötlands Runinskrifter*, 1940, Vol. 5.

13. Wahlgren, p. 142.

14. *Norsk Tidsskrift for Sprogvidenskab*, 1932, pp. 237ff.

15. This letter is preserved in the Minnesota Historical Society Archives, Box 10.

16. Wahlgren, p. 143.

17. Wahlgren, p. 141, bottom of page.

18. This is also shown in his Figure 14.

CHAPTER ELEVEN

1. *Symra*, Decorah, Iowa, 1909, V, 125.

2. P. A. Munch, *Det Norske Folks Historie, Unionsperioden*, I, 579, 612-17.

3. *The Norse Discoverers of America*, 1921, p. 196. See also Wm. Hovgaard, *The Voyages of the Norsemen to America* 1914, pp. 61-64; A. Fossum, *The Norse Discovery of America*, 1918, pp. 80, 91.

4. H. R. Holand, *Explorations in America Before Columbus*, 1956, pp. 282-87.

5. *Nordisk Tidsskrift*, 1950.

6. Klemming's edition, p. 163.

7. Morison, *Admiral of the Ocean Seas*, 1942, p. 649.

8. Archbishop John Ireland in the *St. Paul Dispatch*, Dec. 14, 1909. Also, *Records of the Past*, Vol. IX, 1910. Professor Francis Betten, *From Many Centuries*, 1938, pp. 56-62; Professor James J. Walsh, "The First Prayer in America" in *Columbia*, August, 1933.

9. For explanation of this, see above, Chapter IX, second paragraph.

CHAPTER TWELVE

1. *Della Vita dell' Admiraglio Christ. Columbo,* Venice, 1571, p. 21.

2. *Hist. de Las Indias, Coll. de Documents,* Tom. LXII, p. 99.

3. *Gesta Hamburgensis,* Ch IV, p. 38.

4. The most complete report on Clavus and Greenland is in A. A. Björnbo, "Cartographia Groenlandica" in *Meddelelser om Grönland,* Vol. 48.

5. V. Stefansson's edition of *The Three Voyages of Martin Frobisher,* Vol. 1, p. 19.

6. *Voyages of Captain Foxe and Captain James* (London, 1894), Vol. 2, pp. 332 n., 336-47.

7. Cnoyen's narrative, folio 268 *verso.* Also in E. G. R. Taylor's *Imago Mundi,* p. 60.

8. *The Three Voyages of Martin Frobisher,* Stefansson's edition, 1938, Vol. 1, p. 19.

9. *The Voyages of William Baffin,* 1612-1622, The Hakluyt Society, 1881, p. 128. The map faces p. 103.

10. Vol. 18, 1928, p. 10.

11. See the annotation on the margin of Mercator's map of 1569.

12. See Cnoyen's narrative, folio 268 *verso* or Taylor in *Imago Mundi,* p. 60.

13. Taylor, E. G. R., *Imago Mundi,* p. 64.

14. This was emphasized in 1577 by Captain George Best in the following words: "This so particular a description of the land countries lying about the Pole, argueth that this Oxford frier tooke great pains therein, and induceth great probabilities and liklihood of the truth thereof, bicause be observed so diligently my measure, the bredth of the indrafts, what time, and how long they continued frozen, and with how maney mouths or receipts every one of them received the ocean." *The Three Voyages of Martin Frobisher,* publications of the Hakluyt Society, 1867 edition, Vol. 38, pp. 34 ff.

15. See *Meddelelser om Grönland,* Copenhagen, Vol. 48, Plate 4. The photographic reproduction here shown was prepared by the University library in Oslo. I am indebted to the late Captain Roald Fladmark of the Norwegian Merchant Marine for calling my attention to this map of Hudson Bay.—H.R.H.

16. Alexander Bugge, "Handelen mellom Norge og England," *Hist. Tidsskrift,* Oslo, 1896.

17. *Studier over Vinlandsreiserne,* 1888, pp. 73, 74.

18. J. C. Halliwell, *The Private Diary of John Dee.*

19. Hakluyt's *Voyages,* 1903, pp. 301-4.

20. Exactly 250 years later, Captain William Button and his expedition spent the winter here. Nelson River is named after Francis Nelson, one of Button's officers who died here.

21. British Museum Papers, Taylor's translation, p. 58.

22. *Ibid.*

23. His appointment is printed in *Diplomatorium Norwegicum IV,* p. 341.

CHAPTER THIRTEEN

1. *The Norse Discovery of America,* 1918.

2. *Norse Discoveries of America,* Oxford, 1921.

3. *The Kensington Stone, a Mystery Solved,* p. 78.

4. The letter is dated May 17, 1961.

5. Book II, Ch. 13.

6. *Skandinavien under Unionsperioden,* 1911, pp. 115, 329 n. 8, 330.

7. The substance of this letter was first printed in *Detroit Lakes Record,* August 5, 1943.

8. Wahlgren, p. 79.

9. It is on record that Tosten Torkelson, a neighbor of Ole Bjorndal, caught a wagonload of fish in this lake in 1877, see *Fargo Forum,* June 7, 1939, p. 23.

10. His letter is printed in Holand, *Westward From Vinland,* 1940, pp. 200 f.

11. Professor R. B. Harvey of the University of Minnesota was the first to call attention to this mooring stone. It has now been moved to the runestone monument in Alexandria.

CHAPTER FOURTEEN

1. See his "Discovery of Sauk Valley Man of Minnesota with an account of the Geology," Kirk Bryan, Henry Retzek and Franklin T. McCann; printed in *Bulletin of Texas Archeological and Paleontological Society,* 1938, X, 114-35.

2. This hypothesis was first suggested by my son, Harold Holand.

3. *Catholic Encyclopaedia,* I, 348.

4. "No priest may celebrate the Mass without light [usually two candles] except in case of great urgency." *Ibid.,* X, 20.

5. *Ibid.,* I, 347.

6. *Ibid.,* I, 351.

7. See Holand, *Westward From Vinland,* 229-31, where a fourteenth-century Scandinavian spear is pictured and described. The shank shows that the shaft was a scant inch thick.

CHAPTER FIFTEEN

1. This Frog Point is about six miles northwest of Climax, Minnesota.

2. Letter dated September 7, 1945.

3. For further details about this find, see Holand *The Kensington Stone,* pp. 164-66.

CHAPTER SIXTEEN

1. *Travels into North America,* etc., translated into English by J. R. Forster, London, 1771.

2. His father, René Gaultier, Sieur de la Varennes, a captain in the French army, settled at Three Rivers, Canada, in 1665.

3. See article *Turks,* Language, p. 3.

4. *Inscriptions de l'Orkhon,* published by the Société Finno-Ougrienne, Helsingfors, 1892, Plate 8.

5. I am indebted to Mr. Philip Ainsworth Means for sending me photographs of cuts in Strahlenberg's book.

CHAPTER SEVENTEEN

1. Many of these travelers have left records of their observations, all of which agree in the main concerning the points mentioned in the preceding paragraph. The most important are *Journal and Letters of De La Verendrye,* Toronto: The Champlain Society, 1927; This *Journal* is also printed in Margry, *Découvertes et Etablissements des Fraiņçais,* VI, 585-95; Mc-

Intosh's *Report* (1773) to the U. S. Indian Bureau, summarized in Schoolcraft's *History, Conditions and Prospects,* III, 253-54; *The Manuscript Journal of Alexander Henry* (Elliott Coue's edition, 1806), I, 322-43, 363-66; George Catlin's *North American Indians* (1841), I, 79-184; II, appendix A; Maximilian, Prince of Wied-Neuwied, *Voyage en l'Amérique du Nord* (1834), translated and reprinted in *Early Western Travels,* XXIII, 252-367; XXIV, 11-84; Will and Spinden, *The Mandans,* in *Papers of the Peabody Museum,* III, 85-219.

2. La Verendrye's remarks about the ramparts, bastions and wide ditches are verified by Will and Spinden's excavations, see *op. cit.,* p. 151. See also Bougainville, *Northern and Western Boundaries of Ontario,* p. 83.

3. From La Verendrye's *Journal* (Brymner's translation in *Report on Canadian Archives,* Ottawa, 1889, 1890), p. 3 ff. See also *South Dakota His. Colls.* VII, 340, 341.

4. His report is printed by Gustav Storm, "Venetianerne paa Röst i 1432" in *Det Norske Geografiske Selskabs Aarbog,* VIII, 37 ff. Also printed by Knut Gjerset in his *History of the Norwegian People,* II, 53-60. See also Gudmundsson. *Privatboligen Paa Island,* pp. 90 ff. 105-6. Also Ivar Aaren, *Ordbok,* art. *Kyvetak.*

5. Published by the Smithsonian Institution, 1912, II, 797. It was N. H. Winchell who first suggested the amalgamation of the Norse explorers of 1362. See his *The Aborigines of Minnesota,* 1911, p. 574.

6. George Catlin, *North American Indians,* 1: 177-82. Catlin's veracity of observation and narration are attested to by many persons who had spent much time among the Mandans, such as A. Maximilian and Lewis Cass.

INDEX

201